248.843 DiMarco, Hayley, author.
DIM   A woman overwhelmed

"Hayley D 8\2017 AME know
God more his book
will lead you to laugh, learn, and lean in to the love of God in fresh,
deep, and invigorating ways."
—Gwen Smith
Author of *I Want It ALL* and *Broken into Beautiful*, cofounder
of Girlfriends in God

"In her personality-infused, Scripture-centered style, Hayley
provides help for any woman who wonders about her own circumstances, fears the unknown, or is overwhelmed with life. This book
is a must."
—Alexandra Kuykendall
Author of *Loving My Actual Christmas: An Experiment in Relishing the
Season* and co-hostess of *The Open Door Sisterhood* podcast

"Are you living in a constant state of being overwhelmed? You
don't have to live this way anymore! Allow Hayley DiMarco to come
alongside you as a friend, sharing her struggles and what she's
learned about leaning on the overwhelming love of God."
—Arlene Pellicane
Speaker and author of *31 Days to Becoming a Happy Wife*

A WOMAN OVERWHELMED
FINDING GOD IN THE MESSES OF LIFE

**Library of Congress Cataloging-in-Publication Data
has been requested.**
ISBN 978-1-5018-4070-8

17 18 19 20 21 22 23 24 25—10 9 8 7 6 5 4 3 2 1
MANUFACTURED IN THE UNITED STATES OF AMERICA

CONTENTS

CONTENTS

MY OVERWHELMING INTRODUCTION

I was introduced to a life overwhelmed when I was five years old. My neighbor Sabrina, who coveted my little metal tricycle, decided it had to be hers. So sometime during the night, she opened our adjoining backyard gate, put her dirty little fingers on the handlebars of my red Rocketrike, and yanked it over to her yard by the tassels. When I awoke the next morning, my ride was gone; lifted like a wallet from an unsuspecting tourist.

After searching everywhere, I began to panic. I ran into the house to tell my mom, when I suddenly heard Sabrina yelling from the other side of the fence. "I've got your trike and you aren't getting it back!"

I couldn't believe my best friend in the whole duplex had done this to me. My first reaction was shock, then anger, and then tears. I was completely overwhelmed by this act of border aggression and my inability to open the gate and confront her. So I raced in to get President Mommy: she'd put some executive power behind opening the borders and starting the peace talks.

A few presidential mandates later and Sabrina finally opened the latch on her side of the fence. There she was, standing next to my trike, in the triumphant pose of a conquering hero, rake standing aggressively by her side. Upon seeing this little barbarian grimace, I winced and hid behind my mother's legs. I couldn't advance on the enemy; it was too overwhelming. Smiling at the situation, my mother kindly said, "Sabrina, give her back the trike." And then Mom told me to go over and get it. I walked toward Sabrina like a kid reaching for the broccoli on her plate—nose turned away and eyes squinting in self-protection and disgust—and grabbed the trike.

That was my earliest recollection of being overwhelmed by life. Of course, that was nothing compared to all the other overwhelming things that have happened since then and continue to happen. But now I take comfort in knowing that I am not alone. As it happens, I've never met a woman who wasn't overwhelmed by something. It's a fact of life: us women are overwhelmed by the certainty that our work is never done and that if, by some outside chance it is, someone else's work will be right there begging us to fix it for them.

That's why, in the pages of this book, I have spilled the comical parts of my overwhelming life all over the place for you to laugh at and hopefully see some of yourself within. So don't spend too much time trying to clean things up for me; just relax and go with the flow, knowing that you aren't the only overwhelmed woman in the world. Maybe in seeing something of yourself in the mess of my life, you'll be able to give yourself a break and laugh instead of cry.

You have to know that many of the conditions of my heart are lifelong malfunctions that I have only recently dealt with, and many I am still fighting to this day. But, thankfully, all of them are covered by the redeeming power of the cross. And so

I bring them to you in order to agree with God that I'm in need of a savior, and to thank Him for fulfilling that need.

As you put yourself into the mix with my bad examples and God's good ones, I hope that you will find a way to move from overwhelmed by life to overwhelmed by God—and to go from living the "mission of me" to embracing the mission of Him. I hope you will see that there actually isn't more to do than there is time, and realize that comparison is a deadly habit that makes you more overwhelmed than a woman with only fifty cents at an Everything's-a-Dollar sale.

In the end, I pray that you will find yourself so overwhelmed by the love of God that you won't have the time or desire to be overwhelmed by the circumstances of life. I want to encourage you to see everything through the filter of His love and to understand what that means for your to-do list and your relationships.

So join me in this journey into a life overwhelmed, as we laugh, cry, pray, and go from too much of a bad thing to so much of a good thing that we can't help jumping for joy!

1

ELBOW DEEP
IN BIRTHDAY CAKE

There are a lot of things to be overwhelmed with. I have been overwhelmed with...

worry
fear
 faith
  doubt
 loss
gain
failure
 rejection
  acceptance
   finances
  love
 hate
regret
 responsibility

organization
mess
loneliness
hopelessness
inability
lack
abundance
... and the list could go on.

It's overwhelming how much I've been overwhelmed!

But if I'm honest with myself, I'm not so much over-whelmed with my life as I am with everyone else's. *I'm* doing what I want to do, but *they* aren't doing what *I* want them to do. If everyone would just do what I want them to do, I wouldn't be so overwhelmed. But from my husband and daughter to my friends and enemies, getting people to see that my ways are the best is like trying to convince my dog that he doesn't want to eat my dirty socks. It's a losing battle. Yeah, what I can't control worries me.

I imagine how invigorating it would be if I could just give everyone a list and, without a peep, they would get to work checking things off. Can you imagine the serenity that would give me? I could have my own website with the ultimate master to-do list on it—and every day, my husband could check that site instead of wasting his time on ESPN.com and do all the work on the list.

Hayleyslist.com my dream come true!

If I could, I would even give a list to

> I'm *doing what I want to do,*
> but they *aren't doing what I*
> want them to do. If everyone
> would just do what I want
> them to do, I wouldn't be so
> overwhelmed.

Hollywood producers and tell them which shows to cancel and which to keep. And why stop there? I could give God a list of appropriate weather patterns for my daily activities.

Oh, and I want all drivers to listen when I tell them how to drive!

Step one: *Always use your blinker!*
Step two: *GET OUT OF MY WAY!*
Step three: *And get off my tail!*

Yes, I'm overwhelmed simply because I'm not in charge.

When destiny is under *my* dominion, I feel like an air-traffic controller who hasn't killed anyone in a week. I'm keeping an eye on everyone's location, I'm finding the most efficient air routes, and I'm helping everyone take off and land. But when I'm out of control, planes are dropping out of the sky like flies, and I'm doing all I can just to save one 747 from splatting into the control tower. It's chaos! And it's because of this lack of control that I'm about to send myself to the hospital for psychiatric evaluation—just hoping they'll lock me up so I can finally get some rest! My stomach is aching and I'm popping antacids and diffusing Peace and Calming oil, saying, "Just breathe."

Yes, whatever is out of my control is overwhelming. So my goal in life is to find the best way to control—well, everything. Including my people. No, *especially* my people—at least *they* have to do what I tell them. But, boy, does the ulcer start to flare when they don't!

In a Stress Screener self-test I took online, saying yes to more than four symptoms suggested a real problem with having too much to handle. So no big surprise that I answered yes to eight of them.

Do you struggle with any of the following?

Emotional eating
Insomnia
Digestive problems
Ulcers
Anxiety
Tension headaches
Weight gain
Irritability

When life is more than I can handle—when just looking at it reveals my complete inadequacies and failures, and all I want to do is go back to bed—I know that I am overwhelmed, and not in a good way.

> *It's who we are simply because we are loved by Him, and that reality has to be the most overwhelming thing of all.*

When my body is begging me for a straitjacket and a padded cell, and I'm starting to consider it, I know it's time to reassess my priorities and look for flaws in my logic and planning. I'm tired of being overwhelmed by life. I want something more! Don't you?

THOUGHTS TO PONDER

What overwhelms you? *I ask because I know it's got to be something. Every woman I've ever talked to self-identifies as a woman overwhelmed.*

What is it that makes us so susceptible to the deluge of delusions brought on by the world? *(There has got to be a better way, doesn't there?)*

If you could give up being consumed by two things that overwhelm you, what would they be?

Why do you think they consume you so much?

I'm sorry that you've been overwhelmed by the challenges of life, my friend, but I'm glad that you are here and that you are taking the first steps toward letting go of the crazy. In the pages of this book, I've opened up my life in order to remind you that you are not alone and, in fact, are probably not as crazy as you may think. I hope that as you experience *my* overwhelmed life from the outside in, you will begin to recognize not only yourself but also the truth that we are all so easily overwhelmed, because we were made to be so. It's who we are simply because we are loved by Him, and that reality has to be the most overwhelming thing of all. To be loved by the Creator and Sustainer of everything and everyone, the Great I Am, the King of Kings, and the Lord of Lords, the One who hung the moon and who knew you before you were born, the One who holds the future in His hands. This One who is irresistible to your heart longs to make you a woman overwhelmed with Him and with all the beauty He has placed within and without you.

I pray that God will give you insight into the depths of His love and maybe even a glimpse of the comedy of it all as seen from the rearview mirror, or from the passenger seat of my car. And I pray that, in those things, you will discover freedom. I also hope that you will find the grace to begin to close your worldly eyes to the messiness of life as you open your spiritual eyes to the beauty surrounding that mess. There is a reason that a father takes cute pictures of his baby at those magical moments when she is covered in chocolate pudding or elbow-deep in birthday cake—because in them he sees the joy of his child not only relishing what he's given her, but also diving into it, to the top of her head and the tips of her fingers; covering herself with the goodness that he has supplied. She's not worrying about how to clean it up or thinking, *What a waste!* She's just basking in the abundance.

Today, let us bask in the abundance of the Father. His unfathomable depths can surely replace our fathomable mess.

Can you find out the deep things of God?

Can you find out the limit of the Almighty?

It is higher than heaven—what can you do?

Deeper than Sheol—what can you know?

Its measure is longer than the earth

and broader than the sea. (Job 11:7-9)

2

PREGNANT FOR CENTURIES

My husband, Michael, is the youngest of six kids, who were all born three years apart. I did the math, and figured out that his mother had a baby in diapers for twenty years! Talk about overwhelming!

When we had our daughter, I was so overwhelmed with caring for this creature I knew nothing about, that one night while trying to nurse her in the rocking chair with Michael cheering for me gently at my feet, I said, in all seriousness, "Can we take her back? Do you think it's too late for them to take her back?" He held back a snicker and whispered, "No honey, we cannot take her back. She's ours now." I was deflated. Engulfed in dread and doubt, I was certain this was the worst idea we had ever had.

Then I started to think seriously about the *first* woman overwhelmed, Eve. Can you imagine how overwhelming her future would have looked? "Welcome to the world! This is your husband. He's going to be naming all the animals ever created. And you? You're going to be making all the humans! But don't worry—you've got a lifetime to get it all done. Let's see, at one kid for every year you live, you'll easily pop out eight hundred kids in your lifetime. Piece of cake! Which you'll also need to learn to make and bake, but you can pick that up later. So yeah, you can be pregnant for centuries. But who would be overwhelmed by that?"

Eight hundred years? I remember when I thought thirty-seven years was a long time—a long time to be single! Because that's how long I waited until I finally got my man. I remember thinking, "You've got to be kidding me! My life is almost half over and still nothin'! What are the odds?" I was tired of eating the entire carton of ice cream alone. I wanted someone to watch me, because I wasn't thinking of sharing. I really wanted someone to shop with, because it's not really therapy unless someone else can tell me how cute I look. I wanted a partner to help me pick out furniture, or maybe I should say to just tell me how cute my furniture choices were. (Who am I kidding? Again, a problem with control, but anywhozit . . .) I wanted someone to go on weekend trips to bed and breakfasts with me. Put plain and simply, I wanted a partner. Or maybe I just wanted a BFF—but I wanted her to be a man. I was overwhelmed with loneliness. I was man-hungry and starving to death.

So I opened up the smorgasbord of hot Christian men (that is, Christianmingle.com) and got my scooping hand ready! I loaded up on all kinds of profiles, searching for the perfect one, and it wasn't long before I found him! The ideal guy for me was making a monkey face next to a statue of Rafiki from *The Lion King*, as opposed to all the other guys who were posed next to their sports cars, fighter jets, or ex-girlfriends. (I kid you not!) Reading his profile was like digging out from under the quagmire of loneliness one perfect bio line at a time. The youngest of six kids? Great! There's the perfect ready-made family for this lonely only child. A writer? A speaker? Everything I ever dreamt of in one man! He was the answer to my love needs *and* business needs. I'd marry him and make him my manager (or husbanger), thus filling two voids with one man. Good-bye overwhelmedness!

And, hello…*overwhelmedness!*

Yes, one excess was replaced by yet another. Isn't it funny how that works? My mind went from being consumed with finding a man to being consumed with the man I had found. I can remember being unable to take my eyes off of him. As we drove down the road, I'd put my elbow on the middle console and lovingly balance my chin in my hand (of course, I wasn't driving) as I devoured him with my love-hungry eyes, à la Patrick Swayze and Jennifer Grey. We'd go to a restaurant and I'd jump into his side of the booth so I could touch him, smell him, and stare at him all at once. I was the adoring stalker girlfriend in love with everything about him—even his occasional misstep, or stupid idea. I loved it all. Who wouldn't? He was perfect and he was mine!

Maybe you can tell that when I feel something deeply, I give it a hundred and ten percent. That just means I give it more than I have, which I guess could be the definition of being overwhelmed. Listen, if my heart is a factory of overwhelmedness, it's just because I care so much. But it's true, isn't it? Whether we feel terribly bad or terribly good, both can be overwhelming simply because it's more than we have the mental capacity to bear. And when life is full, so is our ability to live it.

THOUGHTS TO PONDER

We once gave a ridiculous present to our then five-year-old, who was so excited to get her very first iPad that she held it tightly to her chest and ran to her room screaming with joy. "You're welcome!" we both said to her backside as the door slammed shut. She was more excited about the gift than she was about the giver—typical human! (What am I saying? I should say *typical child of mine*. She does have my DNA and, as Winston Churchill said, "I'm easily satisfied with the best.") But the best can be just as overwhelming as the worst. It can consume you, take up all of your waking thoughts, and pepper all of your sleeping ones as well. You don't have to be too busy to be overwhelmed—just too excited to sleep.

It can be hard to find God in the midst of too much of a thing. In fact, too much, by definition, fills every nook and cranny, like my meat and veggies bowl at Mongolian Grill: there ain't no room for another thing! But perhaps we could imitate the apostle Paul who determined in his life that, whatever gain he had, he counted as loss for the sake of Christ. Indeed, he counted everything as loss because of the surpassing worth of knowing Christ Jesus. For the sake of Jesus, Paul suffered the loss of all things and counted them as rubbish in order that he might gain Christ (see Philippians 3:7-8). If we count it all, the good and the bad, as rubbish in comparison to the value of knowing Christ more, then what used to overwhelm can now be put onto the Mongolian grill of life and be made into a sumptuous spread rather than an overwhelming pile of unprepared repast.

Are you willing to lay your goodies down in order to pick up the "goodest" of all—your Savior Jesus Christ?

3

NO WONDER ITALIAN WOMEN THROW PLATES

Yes, I was overwhelmed with hearts and roses and all that is romance—until we said, "I do." Then I took the highway of overwhelmedness that had delivered me from the Land of Isolation to the Kingdom of Love, and exited abruptly into the realm of Are You Kidding Me? That's where I promptly realized that sometimes being overwhelmed makes us blind to everything except that which overwhelms us. When we were dating, those minor differences between us were no big deal but once we were married they

We like to live in the shallow water, where we can't drown in our emotions. We want life to be easy, not messy.

Emotions: messy.

Fun: easy.

became like that tiny grain of sand caught in your eye—annoying and overwhelming beyond its size.

Our first year of *mirage*, as I like to call it, since it was a romance that appeared possible *but was not*, was a disaster: nothing like I thought marriage would be.

Let's just say the seventy-four years of singleness between us had turned us into marital curmudgeons. We were, as you can imagine, "set in our ways" (said in an old grandpa voice), and living together in the same house was like putting metal in a microwave: loud and potentially dangerous.

It was the mix of backgrounds that really got us in trouble. See, I am of Norwegian descent and come from a family that is easygoing and unemotional—we prefer fun over substance. In other words, we like to live in the shallow water, where we can't drown in our emotions. We want life to be easy, not messy. Emotions: messy. Fun: easy.

Michael, on the other hand, is Italian and Irish, which means he's the opposite of Norwegian. He is comfortable with an emotional mess. He loves to talk, even shout, about the messy side of life—you know, about things like love and regret. He wants to analyze problems and conceive of solutions. I prefer a broom and a nice area rug to sweep all my junk under.

So, our first year of marriage went something like this:

> **Michael:** You just stepped on my foot! Don't
> you want to say anything?
> **Hayley:** Yeah! What was your foot doing
> there, right where people walk?

In fact, anytime I hurt him, he wanted me to say "I'm sorry," but I had *never* spoken those words in my life. Speaking them would mean I was wrong, and I don't purposely do things wrong. So technically it was an *accident*, and we don't say sorry for *accidents* over which we have no control. Duh! We are not guilty; therefore, we do not say sorry.

Yes, this little battle took place on a daily basis. He wanted me to confess my mistakes and I wanted him to get over it. He wanted to talk about things of substance and I wanted to go shopping. His fingernails scratching down the chalkboard of my life was nothing like the romance I believed was marriage.

> *There is just no way to be overwhelmed without acting on it.*

Where were the bubble baths and candles? Where were the bedtime foot rubs and the romantic mix tapes?

I jest, but if I had been an atheist, I would have asked for a do-over. We were drowning in our differences and not in a good way. We had made a big mistake! We weren't in love; we didn't even like each other. We raised our voices and slammed our doors as we walked through them.

We were miserable.

And so I was done; done being the quiet Nordic woman who never saw a problem. I was an Italian woman now, with an Italian last name to prove it. So I decided to own my new life and to shout and throw things just like I'd seen Italian women do on TV.

To prepare for my transformation, I went to the local thrift store and bought a bunch of cheap plates. I carried them downstairs to our subterranean garage and piled them on the floor. Then I picked them up, one by one, and threw them at the stone wall. And with each crash, I rose closer to the surface of the ocean of emotion I was drowning in. No wonder Italian women threw plates; it's the only way they could live with Italian men!

Face it: there is just no way to be overwhelmed without

acting on it. In fact, being overwhelmed is like running through the house flipping on all the switches—the lights, the blender, the food processor, the garbage disposal—all at once. Whether you are overwhelmed into silent inaction, loud reaction, or just running in circles like a chicken who just tripped over its own head, your body's systems are all working hard for the money—so hard for it, honey—and one day they're gonna up and quit!

If I had to keep up that stalky love thing I had for Michael in the beginning for more than a year, I would have died. I was too happy to eat and too excited to sleep. My body couldn't keep up at that pace. And later, though the marital trips to the basement let off some steam, my anger engine was still working overtime!

When we are overwhelmed by life, our bodies pay the price. Adrenal exhaustion, chronic fatigue, thyroid problems, ulcers, headaches, body ache, and irritable bowels—all brought to you by an extreme focus on the problem of "too much to do and too little time to do it."

Though the world says we can and should have it all, we just physically cannot, which anyone who's tried to maintain the perfect adrenaline-rushing excitement of new love while building a career and raising a strong and well-bonded family knows. When giving it your all means giving it three hundred percent, it just isn't mathematically possible. And I know the maths, so trust me.

THOUGHTS TO PONDER

I don't recommend you go out and buy old plates. Though I know many women have taken my story as advice, that's not what you should do. It is far better to address the issue than to let off the steam of the symptom. And I pray that's what we can do before this book is over: address the issues that lead to those emotions of anger, bitterness, resentment, and frustration, and rewire your overwhelmed mind to focus on the One who makes this life possible, with all of its emotional lows and rocky mountain highs.

How is it different when you are overwhelmed with the lows than with the highs?

Which emotion do you struggle with the most in relationship to those closest to you?

How is your health suffering from the things that you allow to overwhelm you? (Trust me—it is!)

How is being overwhelmed getting in the way of your relationships, with family, friends, and our Heavenly Father?

One of the most amazing things that God gives us is the ability to grow fruit (the fruit of the Spirit), which is love, joy, peace, patience, kindness, goodness, faithfulness, gentleness, and self-control. (See Galatians 5:22-23.)

These are the products of a life lived in the Spirit and are the very things that can dig us out of our overwhelmedness. Imagine if, in those relationships that overwhelm you, you could respond not with anger, depression, impatience, meanness, and—well, you fill in the blank—but could instead, with only a gentle look toward heaven, offer up the opposite: the fruit of His presence in your life. How would your life be different then?

Let me tell you—hugely!

Yep, the fruit of the Spirit not only gives others a taste of the Savior, but also gives us the sustenance we need to reject those things that feed our overflow of badness, and instead accept those things that fill us with His goodness. But in order to find baskets of Holy Spirit fruit in our lives, we have to want it; and in order to want it, we have to know what *it* is. God's ideas on love, joy, peace, and the rest is oftentimes different than the world's.

Ask God today to begin to teach you about His fruit and how He wants to grow it in your life and relationships. The more abundant His fruit, the less abundant your worries.

I

SO MUCH TO DO,
SO LITTLE TIME

4

IT'S ALL A SCAM TO SELL US MORE MAGAZINES!

I remember when I turned seventeen, and suddenly there was a magazine just for me. It was the coming of age publication that knew everything about... well everything! I literally waited until my seventeenth birthday to buy my first copy of *Seventeen* magazine. I felt like such a grown-up handing the clerk $1.25 for my all-expenses-paid trip to womanhood, featuring Brooke Shields—or was it Phoebe Cates? Whoever it was, she was A-M-A-Z-I-N-G!

I took that beauty home, lay down on my bed, and opened up the world that is *Seventeen*. I read every page, including the letter from the editor. I've never learnt as much as I learnt that day. Had I been living under a rock? I didn't know what foreign boys thought of American girls, or what my RQ (romantic quotient) was—that is, until *Seventeen* taught me.

I learned the A to Z of skincare and six essential makeover tips. I found out how to protect my body from harmful UV rays and what to put on my hair to make it sun-bleached.

> *You've heard of over-achievers? Yeah, not one of those. I'm an over-reactor. I like to swing the pendulum as far to one side as it was on the other.*

It was so meaty and I was so hungry that it took me two hours to read the thing. By the time I was done, I was dying to try it all out.

I did that all over again for the next few months, until I finally decided to go for broke and get my first subscription. *Exciting!* But my beauty bible started coming quicker than I could get through it, and my bathroom started to look like the makeup counter at Macy's after a Black Friday sale—strewn with half-used cosmetics, lotions, and cotton balls. My morning and bedtime rituals went from changing my clothes and brushing my teeth to a half-hour of plucking, powdering, primering, protecting, and painting. It was exhausting, but I was able to do it, and boy did it show! I went from a sweet little Cindy Brady look-a-like to sexy Farrah Fawcett wanna-be in one summer. When I got back to school, no one knew who I was—literally. The perm and the change of hair and makeup had everyone thinking I was the new girl, and I loved it.

But then one day, many years later, I read an article in another magazine that changed everything. The journalist who wrote it had collected all of the beauty tips touted by women's magazines, assigned times to them, and then added up how long it would take a woman to do them all. It came out to something like five hours a day.

After reading this sober truth, I slowly sat the magazine down as if I had just read in Revelation 23:1 the words, "Ha ha, just kidding!"

I screwed up my face and considered the lie I had been believing all my years as a young woman: that I could do it all.

"I can't do it all," I said in agreement with the journalist. "It's a scam to sell us more magazines!"

Over the next few days, every time I thought about removing my eye makeup or plucking my eyebrows, I just didn't. It was all too much for me to bear. I was suddenly overwhelmed by the knowledge that there wasn't enough time in the day, and so I froze. I gave up trying. I quit doing everything: washing my face, hydrating my skin, all of it. You've heard of over-achievers? Yeah, not one of those. I'm an over-reactor. I like to swing the pendulum as far to one side as it was on the other.

Fast forward ten years, and I had now—not surprisingly—become overwhelmed yet again, but in the opposite direction. I was now overwhelmed by the condition of my hair and skin, which I had let go because they were entirely too overwhelming to maintain. Seriously, when I woke up to the fact that perhaps moderation was the answer, I had just been booked on Fox News in New York to talk about my book *Mean Girls*. I needed a quick pick-me-up out of my frumpy rebellion from hygiene, so I found a salon in the Yellow Pages (Kickin' it old school!) and got myself an appointment.

I went from a mousy, split-end-infested, long-blonde nobody, to a golden-blonde, graduated-bob-wearing trendsetter in under three hours. The follicle refinement was so fabulous, the stylist said she was sad she hadn't snapped before-and-after pics. And when I went to New York, the host of the show was so blown away by the cut that she asked her stylist to give her my exact hairstyle. *What? She's back, baby!*

I had given up on myself completely because I was overwhelmed with too much to do every day. But after over-compensating for the mistaken idea that I needed to do it all, I decided moderation would be less overwhelming. I just *had* to do something. Now, ten years later, I'm still trying to play catch-up, little by little, for all those years of disrepair. But I'm a lot better off than if I'd just kept avoiding everyday upkeep—like a renter who has no eyes for the dilapidation of her shack—because I was just too overwhelmed.

THOUGHTS TO PONDER

Have you ever been overwhelmed into inaction? A common reaction to having too much to do is to do nothing at all. That's because the first step's a doozy! If you've ever said, "I just don't know where to start," you've probably been overwhelmed into inaction.

What in your life seems too hard to tackle?

What is one thing you could do toward that goal this week?

What victories have you had in the past when facing a big challenge?

Are you more overwhelmed by *how much* you have to do or *what* you have to do?

Size doesn't determine possibility. In fact, God is very fond of giving impossibly huge jobs to impossibly unqualified people. It's His M.O. If He gave easy jobs, then no one would see Him at work; but the bigger the job, the more obvious it is that you couldn't have done it by yourself.

Most of the time, the very thing that overwhelms us is the thing He wants to take a major part in doing. All He asks is that we get moving: walk around the wall, rally the people, fling the stone, preach the gospel, make disciples. He does the rest. Proverbs 21:31 says, "The horse is made ready for the day of battle, but the victory belongs to the Lord." And in Proverbs 16:9 it says, "The heart of man plans his way, but the Lord establishes his steps."

My paraphrase of these two verses in Proverbs is, "the schedule is planned, but the Lord decides how it will get done." We need to get up and get moving, but we need to be ready for Him to change what we thought we were going to do.

5

IF THERE IS NO ONE TO IMPRESS, THEN THERE WILL BE A MESS

I crave order, but attaining it is like asking a baboon to give birth to a bobcat. It's daunting, destructive, and disappointing all at the same time. I hate chaos, but it's my natural system, and it is a system.

In fact, there must be expected guests in order for there to be concentrated cleaning in my house. Without this social inspiration, there is no gust for my sails, no steam for my engine, no donkey for my cart. It's a simple fact of old-timey nature.

If there is no one to impress, then there will be a mess.

It's true. As desperately as I crave order on the inside, outside I'm a powerless victim of the constant creep of my collection of crap.

Of course, I don't blame it on myself; I blame it on the

architect who designed this cabin we live in. I have what professional organizers call "nowhere to put anything." I have no linen closet, no coat closet, no pantry, no storage closet. What else is there to do but pile stuff on whatever empty surface I can find?

"A place for everything and everything in its place." That's a lie! I've looked. There is not a place for everything.

That's why I designed my patented Shell Game Method. Whenever I get tired of my dining room table being more craft counter than dinner destination, I simply gather all my supplies and hide them in another room. In fact, that is the key to my mess-management methodology: when the mess gets too much, move it. And boy do I do a lot of moving!

"Guests coming tonight, honey? OK, let me move these bags of dog food from the living room into the laundry room."

"Looking for the iron? I'll put my dirty-clothes bins in the garage and pile my shoes on the dryer."

"Where can we eat? Let's move the sewing machine from the dining room table onto the entertainment center, and put my reams of fabric on the couch. We can move them back later."

I am a neat freak trapped in a messy person's body, and I desperately want out!

Movement gives the neat freak in me something to do.

A few years ago, there were these pictures traveling the web of the workspaces of some of the most successful and famous men in the world. I remember the images of Albert Einstein and Steve Jobs the most. Their desks looked like a white-collar crime scene: piles of papers, books, and equipment strewn about the room as if thugs had been tasked with finding the last will and testament of their deceased crime bosses.

Ironically, viewing these mountains of mess made me feel

both uncomfortable and unrestrained. I don't want permission to live in a dump, but I wish I could feel as free as these men did to put the passion of their hearts over the position of their stuff. And that's what it is, isn't it? Permission. If only I could get permission to live in the mess that is life, then I'd feel a lot better.

Life is messy. And running around trying to keep it constantly tidy is like putting your paint and brushes away after every stroke. It might be tidy but your art will suffer.

One day I was running around hiding stuff when my ten-year-old said, "Why are you doing that? Don't you want people to know a kid lives here?" She was right—a little mess is just evidence that life is being lived. I'd like to think that I prioritize children over checklists and that, like tithing the first ten percent of my income, I give the best parts of my time to the people who count instead of to the counters that pile.

The trouble is, I can get so committed to my checklist that I miss those Holy Spirit moments that have so much more eternal value than my perfectly planned and put-away life. I'm not ready to run with my inner hoarder just yet, but I am ready to look at my mess as the evidence of a priority that is shifting from moving stuff around to loving the people around me. I never want to say, "Just let me clean this up before I love you." That's the kind of dysfunction that turns a little girl into an obsessive-compulsive woman. That's the kind of bondage I want freedom from. Yet that's the kind of thing my inner neat freak is screaming in my head. Meanwhile, my new-creature self turns away from the dirty dishes to run and get ice cream with my lovies.

THOUGHTS TO PONDER

Are you a neat freak or a messy?

No matter your answer, I encourage you to tell yourself today that when you fail at your mission, that is just you moving toward moderation and away from being a slave to your personality. Personalities aren't meant to forever stay the same, but to grow and blossom, as each day adds to the confirmation that God's glory is the only glory you are interested in. You are a new creature not only once, but every day that you wake up.

By way of inspiration, think about the ways God has changed you in just the past twelve months. What has He taught you or opened your eyes to? How has He blessed you or saved you from something?

Do you have ability to say no to your schedule in order to say yes to the requests of those you love? Which parts of your schedule do you feel you cannot afford to interrupt? Why?

In what ways could you show your family and friends that they take priority over your need for your previously laid plans?

What is one thing that someone you love keeps asking for but that you are too busy to do? Is there a way you can love that person by denying yourself this week?

It all comes down to how we love, not how we git 'er done. "But gittin 'er done feels like the most loving thing I can do," you reason. And that might be true. But the end never justifies the means, and if the means of gittin 'er done is making you overwhelmed with worry, anger, frustration, and the like, then God may just want you to let it go. He wants you to be able to sing, "The list doesn't rule over me anymore!"

In order to remind myself how to love, I penned these words inspired by 1 Corinthians 13:

> If my house is immaculate, but I have not love, I am but a sounding car alarm that won't shut off.
> And if I have the ability to do it better than anyone else so I just do it myself, and if I have the bargaining skills to get the lowest possible prices, but have not love, I am useless.
> If I upcycle all our old furniture and sell all my used clothes at consignment, and if I give up all my addictions, but have not love, I've gained nothing.
> Love is patient with difficult people and kind to those who don't deserve it;
> love does not want what it doesn't have, or brag about what it does; it is not bossy or blunt. It does not insist on being in control; it's not irritable when interrupted or resentful of having too much to do and not enough time to do it; it does not feel happy when other people prove themselves inferior, but rejoices when they do it better.
> Love bears all messes, accepts all apologies, hopes all change is possible, endures all disrespect and rejection.
> Love never ends.
> As for immaculate houses, they will crumble; as for the ability to do it better than

29

everyone else, forgetfulness; as for getting the best deal, scam artists. For we know today's BOGO and how to clean a house in part, but when the eternal home comes, the temporary one will pass away.

When I was a teenager, I like spoke like a teenager, I like thought like a teenager, and I was like superior like a teenager. When I became a woman, I saw how little I knew before.

Even now, we proclaim wisdom over beauty, but then we will see how little we know now. Now I know a good bit; then I shall know it all, even as I have been known completely.

So now faith, hope, and love last forever. These three; but the greatest of these is love.

That puts it into perspective for me, and stings like a sweat bee caught in the crook of my arm. Because I don't often think about love as having priority over everything else.

Perhaps you feel the same sting. If you do, know that the overwhelming sense of missing the mark and not living up to what you think you should be isn't the quiet voice of God condemning you, but the sulking sound of the flesh believing in its own perfection. We have to allow Christ to be our perfection and we have to rest in the knowledge that *it is finished*— even if our list lies unfinished and begs to be done.

When love is the number one priority, all those negative emotions are squeezed out and the result is rest and a peace that passes all understanding.

Can you rest in that love today whether your list is done or not?

6

THE WORLD CAN'T HANDLE MY NINJA

Have you ever seen one of those chefs at a hibachi grill masterfully flinging double-fisted knives into the air?

And have you seen him use a spatula like a cricket bat to flick shrimp off the grill into the mouth of the guy wanting to impress with his seal-like food-catching skills?

Now, envision the same scenario, but with the diners squealing in self-protection as they witness not shrimp flying toward the open-mouthed customer but the spatula, just after the chef accidentally releases it on the upswing.

That is the image of my relationship with solid objects.

I'm cooking.

I'm cooking.

And out of nowhere, the spatula just *jumps* right out of my hand.

It's like that with all inanimate objects in my presence. I can reach for a spoon in the silverware drawer, and as I'm lifting it out of its little spoon cell, it makes a break for it, jumping out of my hand and over the side of the drawer. I chase it in hot pursuit, touching it occasionally only to change its trajectory but never to grasp it. It happens all the time!

At least once a day, I open up my kitchen cupboard, and as I reach for, say, a bottle of cinnamon, the garlic salt (with its lid half-open because I put it away so quickly last time), jumps right onto the counter, crashing into my bowl of fried apples and ruining the whole thing.

I'm sure you're saying, "You should just catch it before it falls." Just forget about me catching anything, and you'll save yourself a lot of disappointment. In fact, there is a fifty-fifty chance that when you "hand" me something, it's going to end up the same as if you'd dropped it. Hence the need for these constant words to my husband: "Do not let go of this…until I tell you…that I have it." Because whatever it is, it's going to try and make a break for it as soon as it senses my presence.

> *I get so overwhelmed with the slow pace of the world that I want to scream.*

And it's not just about catching things. I once opened the driver's seat door to my van after shopping, and as I turned to sit down, I missed the seat and literally slid onto the step.

Inanimate objects—they see me coming and they run in the opposite direction.

Now it has occurred to me that I'm a quick mover, and that might be part of the problem.

It takes you ten minutes to wash dishes? I can do it in two!

I'm not saying I get them completely clean, but they are good enough to go into a dimly lit cabinet.

And when I have multiple things to do, I've got them all cued up in my mental to-do list so that I'm reaching for the mirror as soon as my fingers touch the brush. That could explain why I drop so much stuff—my brain is too far ahead of my body. It's like when I type something and the computer literally can't keep up with me, so I have to wait for all the letters to slowly show up on the screen. My mind is just too fast: the world can't handle my ninja-like speed.

And that's where I get into trouble. I get so overwhelmed with the slow pace of the world that I want to scream. No matter what I'm doing, it's like I'm late to pick up my lottery winnings and there are fifteen zombies in front of me in a narrow hallway, slowly shuffling instead of actually lifting their feet and walking like normal people. I can't get around them, so I'm stuck behind, flapping my futile wings and watching my millions slip away.

I don't have time for this, people! I've got a schedule to keep.

I just wish the world would find its fast-forward button. I can't wait for people and their "Sunday drives" and "friendly conversation," when action is required. This became especially evident when I moved to the South.

Growing up in Oregon, things were a lot different. Oregonians are more time-conscious like I am. But Southerners are more about kindness and social graces and all that stuff that just sucks the time out of my day and leaves me with nothing but ten minutes to do two hours' worth of work.

I remember when I first learned that you had to socialize with a person *before* you could ask him or her to do something for you. *How do you run a business that way?* I thought. *It's not a date; it's work. Let's save the scintillating conversation for the weekend.*

Yeah, I'm sure I was like a cold glass of water in the face of everyone I worked with. And I'd like to say that I've grown, that I've slowed down and matched the genteel Tennessee pace, but there are still days when I'm sure it looks like I'm the Flash and the rest of y'all are Betty White pushing a walker. Waiting is a bully blocking the bathroom door when I need to pee. And he's making me mad because he's messing with my schedule!

My schedule is "ma'thing."

It's the thing that I commit to each morning. It's the daily devotional I study and prepare to follow so that I can achieve my goals in a timely fashion. Without the schedule, where would I be?

I'd be out of control, that's where I'd be—and then what would the world do without me?

THOUGHTS TO PONDER

So are you shaking your head at my crazy or can you relate? Do you find that people often slow you down? If so, perhaps you struggle a bit with impatience like me. And let's face it, when life doesn't go as planned, it's overwhelming. And it can feel like everything and everyone is against you.

So what makes you impatient?

How do you feel about your schedule?

Do you believe that God gave you too much to do in the time he's given?

How do you feel when you are not in control of your schedule?

Impatience is a need for speed. We've got too much to do and not enough time to do it, and that's a breeding ground for stress, worry, and frustration. But God offers us relief in His patience.

Patience is a gift of the Holy Spirit for anyone who will look for it.

What did Jesus say? "Knock and I will answer." (Matthew 7:7.) When we knock on someone's door, it's because they have something we want, whether that

> *I may never know why God slows me down when He does, but I want to find the strength to trust Him in those times.*

be a cup of sugar, a friendly conversation, or an answer to why their dog keeps pooping on our grass. And when we knock on the door that Jesus wants to open, He has a heaping handful of patience and a soft recliner to put our feet up on, while He takes time by the edges and stretches it out like a piece of taffy.

Time truly is in His hands, and as the old preacher once said, "There is too much for me to do today not to start off with prayer."

Being perpetually engaged to our schedule is sometimes like being engaged to the enemy when God wants us to elope with the Spirit.

The schedule gives us our script, while abiding in Christ feels more like improv. He shows us "whose line it is anyway" in those surprise moments when the studio audience gives us a crazy scenario to act out. He reveals what is important to Him as He interrupts our to-do's and our schedules with the unexpected. I wish I could remember that every time the nurse says, "The doctor will be right with you" and then leaves me in that little windowless room for forty-five minutes.

I don't see the potential for Holy Spirit improv in those situations. I just see no reason for me to miss my next meeting in order to practice my thumb-twiddling while I stare at that "No Cell Phones" sign on the wall. But if God is truly sovereign, if He is all-powerful and all-knowing, love itself, as I know He is, then perhaps His reasons for keeping me secluded are good. Maybe He wants me to trust Him with my time and to give it to Him freely.

I may never know why God slows me down when He does, but I want to find the strength to trust Him in those times, because I know He's gonna continue to do it. I know that He's going to find ways to get me to slow down so that I notice the things that are important to Him and don't get so focused on the things that are so important to me.

If I were all-powerful, all-knowing, and always present, then I could understand scheduling every minute of my life, but I am clearly not any of those things. So I want to leave margin for the One who is, so that He can improvise with my life and teach me to love impulsively.

Today, I'm praying for God to give me the patience to trust Him with my schedule and with that bully called Waiting.

II

DEATH BY COMPARISON

7

LIFE IS LIKE AN ETSY SHOP

She's that perfect specimen of a woman that all good Christian women should compare themselves to.

The amalgam of everything perfect in the world.

You've read about her in Scripture; maybe you've even seen her in the wild as she hands her five-inch stack of coupons to the clerk in front of you, or displays her toilet-paper-roll art on Pinterest.

If you've heard of this woman, then you will recognize her in my Overwhelmed Woman's version of Proverbs 31.

Now, hear me out: I believe the Bible is a great source of relief, hope, and inspiration. But, if I'm being honest, this particular chapter in the Old Testament has become a great source of comparison for many a woman, thanks to our preoccupation with perfection.

See, this is what I believe we all imagine when we read Proverbs 31:

Listen up, men: this woman is impossible to find. Finding her is like finding the Hope Diamond in your backyard. But I'm going to tell you about her anyway, so you can compare all other women to her. Finding her will make your life a living paradise.

First of all, she's not afraid of hard work—she likes it! She'll go to Aldi, Safeway, and Publix all in one day just to save you money! In the morning, she'll rise with the birds to feed you: pancakes, bacon, eggs, omelets—anything you and the kids desire. She'll have it laid out like a Hilton buffet.

After breakfast and a quick tilling of the garden, she'll start getting to work flipping houses. While the contractors are taking care of the big stuff, she'll take a break and work on her Etsy business called Knitting Pretty, where she sells chunky, homemade, knit blankets and other crafts she whips up as she rides her stationary bike and sweats to the oldies.

During lunch, she'll serve the homeless at the shelter downtown, even if there is four inches of snow on the ground.

When she gets home, it's time to tackle sewing that new suit you need by Wednesday and making a memory quilt, which takes her into the wee small hours of the morning to complete.

When she rises a few hours later, she quickly loads the minivan with her upcycled palette furniture she's delivering to the boutique down the street. She drives off laughing at the future and praising God for her wonderful life.

> Lunchtime is her weekly Bible study,
> where she teaches and disciples five women
> to become industrious and joyful. Now, she
> might not be charming or beautiful, but her
> hard work certainly will give you something
> to brag about. All that beauty stuff passes
> anyway, but her works will live on forever. She
> is greatly to be praised.

All I can say is thank God that Proverbs 31 isn't addressed to women and how hard they should work, but to the men looking for women who work hard. Otherwise, I'd have to get to work building my business and learning to knit! Of course, we women can use this poem as inspiration for an industrious life—and being the overachieving approval junky that I am, I looked at it as a challenge when I first got married. I took the "excellent wife" thing to the extreme. Appearances being so important to me, I decided my wifey wardrobe must include lots of cute aprons and perky housecoats from the 1950s. I even tried my hand at selling designer handbags I got for bargain prices at Goodwill. (Though, surprisingly—or as my husband would say, "as expected"—no one wanted them.) I also attempted to upcycle old clothes into artsy bohemian tops to sell on my Etsy shop. I mean Etsy flop. (You get the picture.)

Seriously, I agonized over being the perfect wife for years, thus learning that when you are overwhelmed with perfection, you spend more energy regretting what you can't do than doing what you can.

Now, I call it "thirty-one proverbs" instead of Proverbs 31, taking on the opinion of gifted scholars who say this chapter refers to a *collection* of honorable women and not just *one* super-human robot. I'm leaning more toward the Borg model, for my *Star Trek* friends, which says that we are all a part of the hive and meant to hold one another up with our "hive minds."

> *Unfortunately, our desire to impress can end up being our unreason-able target to aim for.*

In other words, we can't do it all ourselves; we need each other, sister! I sure know I do. I need you to remind me that I'm unique and don't have to keep up with all my Facebook friends because I wasn't meant to follow them, but to follow the One who made me. When I look at the perfect, modern Proverbs 31 woman, I am overwhelmed, but when I look at who God made me to be, a little of that trepidation disappears.

Let me tell you that there is nothing more overwhelming than comparison—judging yourself based on who someone else is, is like using an iPhone all your life and then being handed an Android. It isn't going to work the same, and you're just gonna end up throwing it at the wall.

Life is like an Etsy shop where no one is manufactured to exact specifications. Each one of us is uniquely handcrafted, so that no two are the same—giving us all an unequaled, uncommon, and unusual purpose. Our life is not meant to overwhelm us; instead, our life is meant to overwhelm the world with the Creator's amazing grace.

THOUGHTS TO PONDER

Do you often compare yourself with others?

If we can be honest and peel away the layers of the onion that is our life, we can see that most of the things that overwhelm us were born in the comparison center of the brain, where we parade all that we are alongside all that the world shows us we aren't, and begin making up for the differences. That's why a checklist makes so much sense for our daily routine—it gives us a grab-bar we can use to pull ourselves up to where we believe the rest of the world is already hanging over us.

What activities lead you to the slippery slope of comparison?

What gives you the desire to compare yourself to others?

Is there a true standard we are all meant to live up to? Explain.

What if you fail to live up to that standard? How do you deal with that failure?

How would life be for you if you knew that everyone else was worse off than you? Would that change your aspirations or objectives?

Did you know that everyone *is* as bad off as you, if not worse?

Unfortunately, our desire to impress can end up being our unreasonable target to aim for.

If only we could all be honest about our failures, our heartaches, and our feelings, how much would that benefit those who feel like they are alone in their overwhelmed lives? When we attempt to act like we have it all together, we are deceiving others into believing that God didn't have to save us from anything, because we are good enough without Him. The truth is that all of us have been saved by His grace from our repeated failure and stupidity…failure and stupidity, failure and stupidity.

When we aren't bold enough to be transparent with others, we miss out on sharing the amazing redemptive power of Christ with sinners like ourselves. Sometimes, offering grace to others is just about being free to talk about the messiness of our lives and the saving grace of our Savior's death.

So, let my stupid mistakes and incredible failures be a confirmation of the grace that God has offered me and the distance I have traveled thanks to His goodness and mercy. Allow my story to be a comfort to you that Jesus came to seek and save the overwhelmed and not the underwhelmed.

"If you could perfect your life through to-do lists and constant planning, then Christ died for no purpose." (Overwhelmed Woman version of Galatians 2:21)

We know Christ died to save you—not just for heaven, but from living this life overwhelmed by the things He wants to enable you to overcome. As He said, "In the world you will have tribulation. But take heart; I have overcome the world" (John 16:33). And He will overcome the world in you as well.

8

I SEE PERFECT PEOPLE AND THEY WON'T SHUT UP

Becoming the perfect woman might not even be on your radar. You might be thinking, *I'm so overwhelmed with how much I have to do just to make it through the day, I don't have the time or energy to even look at the Proverbs 31 woman.*

You run from one required activity to the other like a downstairs maid in an English abbey. You are more overwhelmed by your to-do list than by your abundance of side businesses and Pinteresting projects. You wonder how women find the time for such luxuries.

You are overwhelmed with fatigue, frustration, resentment, chaos, disorder, and lack. There just isn't enough of you to go around. Talk about overwhelming—you're like a size 2 swimsuit being squeezed onto a size 12 woman. Stretched thin and probably ripping at the seams.

Yes, I think the most overwhelming thing for a lot of women is the to-do list. But for me, it's more about my "what-not-to-do-list." I frankly work much better with negative inspiration than positive. Tell me what not to do and I'm like Gail Carson Levine's main character in *Ella Enchanted*—unable to disobey. I just love the law! It's so neat and tidy, and when I obey it I get an A-plus! Nanny-nanny boo-boo!

Of course, it can be overwhelming having to be perfect all the time, but I believe that perfection suits me better than the alternative. So I run myself ragged trying to collect enough stickers to fill my obedience chart before anyone else: A-plus!

I often describe myself to others as competitive. It's funny how you can say to people without embarrassment, "I'm just really competitive," when what that really means is, "I'm better than you, and if I can't prove it, then I'm going to get really mad."

It's true too! Get me into a big game of Catch Phrase! or Taboo—any word game really—and I go from Piglet to Tigger in six seconds flat. I might as well be singing, ". . . and the most wunnerful thing about Hayley is I'm the only one! I-Y-F-L! In Your Face, Loser!"

Competition feeds the inner savior. You know her—the one who proves to yourself and everyone else that you are worthy of love, attention, and respect. "There are some things only money can buy," she says, "but for everything else, there's competition!" I mean, I'll compete even if no one else is around. All I have to do is

> *There are two results of comparing yourself with another human being*: pride *and* depression.

keep a running tally of others' beauty, cleanliness, kids' performance, job status, and possessions, and it's like *The Game of Thrones*—*Christian Edition* all day long.

I look at my walls and I'm overwhelmed by how ugly my arrangements are compared to Kallie's. Or I'm getting ready for bed and want to leave the kitchen counter cluttered until morning, but then I think of how Jen avoids the kitchen-hoarding horror by never leaving it for later, and I'm torn between rest and overwork.

I remember when Catherine once told me, "I read this blog that said if it takes you less than fifteen minutes to put something away, you should do it now." Now I can't get those words out of my head. I'm like the kid from *The Sixth Sense*, only I'm saying, "I see perfect people and they won't shut up."

Comparison is how we decide most things in our lives. In order to understand something, you have to have something to compare it to. I get that. But there are two results of comparing yourself with another human being: *pride* and *depression*. Neither one ends well. Besides, being the best is hard work, and I know this from personal experience. If I'm being honest—and I most definitely am—in my own mind, I am the best in comparison to everyone else. My body just can't seem to translate that to reality. Whenever I take the time to balance the books of my life, I see more red ink than black, more debt than surplus. In fact, I'm completely overdrawn and bouncing personal checks right and left. Just ask my husband.

Yeah, I'm a lot better in my own mind than in the minds of those who know me best, at least when it comes to what I *think* I should be. And, in fact, that's another reason I get so overwhelmed—because I compare myself not only to others, but also to my "best me." So when I see my best me with her feet up, eating bonbons, and taking "me" time, I'm one woman down. It's unfair, so I just throw my hands up and say, "I can't do it all! It's just too much!" And that signals the end.

Laundry Pile–7
Hayley–0
Game over.

I'll try again tomorrow. Yeah, comparison sucks!

THOUGHTS TO PONDER

Well now that I've exposed my dark underbelly so much that you can probably see my stretch marks, maybe you can also see yourself in my crazy. I hope so, because then I'm not so lonely. But just because we are crazy doesn't mean we have to keep doing the same thing over and over again, hoping we'll get a different response. That would be what psychologists call just plain crazy.

Today is the chance for us to take stock of our comparison muscle and to give ourselves permission to feed it chocolate and send it on vacation.

Are you competitive? If not, why not?

How does it feel when you lose?

What is one area in your life where you most wish you were like someone else?

What is the thing you think you should be better at than you are?

What is the main thing you think about when you are overwhelmed?

Comparison really does serve a good purpose, as we see in Hebrews 6:12, which prompts us to be "imitators of those who through faith and patience inherit the promises."

But, like a lot of things, we wrongly use comparison when we use it to grade ourselves and others rather than inspire faithfulness. Jon Bloom agreed with me (even though he doesn't know me), when he said, "We can tell this is happening in us when we look at others and don't see the grace of

God, but reflections of our own inferiority. We don't see them as windows into God's glory, but as mirrors into which we are asking, 'Who's the fairest one of all?'—and we know it's not us."[1]

I know it's hard to walk past a window and not look at yourself—we are all very interested in how we look—but if we could only remember to look *through* the window to the inside, instead of stopping at our reflection, we could see the very spirit of God alive within us, giving us all that we need for life and even godliness (see 2 Peter 1:3). In fact, if you make the resolve to stop comparing, then you can know that He will fulfill "every resolve for good and every work of faith by his power" (2 Thessalonians 1:11).

Did you get that? He will bring it to pass by His power. Ah, the bonbons of grace. Now sit back and enjoy.

NOTE

1. Jon Bloom, "Lay Aside the Weight of Prideful Comparison," Desiring God website, September 13, 2013, www.desiringgod.org/articles/lay -aside-the-weight-of-prideful-comparison.

9

HE PUT THE PUN
IN PUNISHMENT

Even though what William of Ockham said some seven hundred years ago is probably true—that "The explanation requiring the fewest assumptions is most likely to be correct"—I always prefer to go with the more complicated and time-consuming explanation. I don't know why I'm so dysfunctional like that, but I like to blame it on my past. It's just easier that way and less convicting.

For example, I was taught at an early age to be disappointed by people. Try turning out normal when that's your premise.

People, according my mother, were all double agents. Oh, they may pledge their allegiance to you, but their true loyalty lies behind enemy lines. She got this fantastic training from the self-confidence-inspiring, life-enhancing "bible" called *Looking Out for #1*. I can remember her reading that little handbook and teaching me the mantra, "Look out for yourself, because no one else will!" And with these life-contesting words, the path to Assumption Land became a beaten one.

The world was out to get me. And "the world" included those people I loved or hoped would love me. *They were the worst!*

Take my dad for example—not to be trusted!

An expert on negative reinforcement *with a twist*, he's always using humor to cut people down and "inspire" them to work harder. You could say that my dad puts the *pun* in *punishment*.

A cowboy by trade, Dad is always surrounded by girls—not because they love cowboys, which they just might—but because girls are usually the best horseback riders. And the best horseback riders want to be taught by the best. And he's the best! But to be "inspirational," he "encourages" his students using exaggerated falsehoods to compare them with other, more qualified individuals.

In other words, he mocks them into improvement.

For example, if a girl is running the poles (a series of six poles in a line that the horse weaves through twice), and knocks over two of them (that's bad), he will say something like, "That's not bad. For a girl!" And since these girls are not his daughters, and they are smart enough to know that girls ride much better than boys and that he's just "punishing" them, they simply laugh and try again.

And he's had great results with these high schoolers. In fact, they are cleaning up at horseshows all over the states of Oregon and Washington . . . and I don't mean manure, I mean first-prize belt buckles and saddles. But his results with his own flesh and blood were not always so award-worthy.

One time, when I was ten-years-old, I was mucking stalls. It is what it sounds like:

> muck,
> yuck,
> suck.

I hated every minute of it. And so, like any good little girl, I registered a complaint with the foreman.

My dad, inspiring me to new heights, told me to "Be a man!" He thought nothing of these three words, but I thought of nothing else for the next ten years as I attempted to take on what I thought my dad should do for Mom and me. And then their divorce made it possible: I became the man of the house.

And what do men do?

They fix things.

So I fixed things! I changed light bulbs, I rehung doors, I even changed the starter in my '66 Mustang! All the while resenting him for making me do it. Which he never really did. But hey, I gave him the chance to help by calling him up and asking him *how* to change a starter. But did he make the two-hour drive to our house and change it for me? Or pay for me to take it into the shop? Nope! He just told me how to change a starter!

OK, maybe I could have *asked* him to do it, but I had learnt from my mom and grandmother to assume the worst in him. After all, "he couldn't be trusted" and "he wouldn't do anything for me," so I assumed the worst. And that's just what I got: the worst father-daughter relationship you could have. One where I hated him so much, I changed my last name. Assumptions are great!

Imagine my surprise when, thirty years later, I discovered that my learned impression of him wasn't right, but was just the manure of my imagination. Ugh! That stinks!

How many years I wasted allowing three words—"Be a man"—to overwrite everything I knew about the world and to overflow like a swollen river into the highways and byways of my life!

All those years, I thought that my dad had wanted to have a boy and not a girl. I thought "Be a man" had really meant "I wish you'd been born a boy." But the truth that I came to see is that he actually prefers females to males, because he loves teaching people to ride, and girls learn quicker and win more often than boys.

That means I lived the majority of my life thinking he was against me, when he was really for me. When you make just one assumption about who you are based on what sinful man does or says to you, it's like building your house on the beach. Everything is suntan lotion and romance novels until the waves come in and the sand starts to slide out from under you.

THOUGHTS TO PONDER

It's human nature to assume the worst when people hurt you. Oftentimes, we assign the blame to ourselves when it was no fault of our own. But this kind of response to the words or actions of others makes us approval junkies.

How have you been hurt by someone you loved?

How has that past experience overwhelmed your present?

How have your feelings about it changed over time?

If you could say anything to that person today, what would it be?

Galatians 1:10 has been a constant reminder to me in times of disappointment and rejection. When I have these negative feelings in relationship to others, I ask myself the same thing Paul asked himself: "Am I now seeking the approval of man, or of God? Or am I trying to please man? If I were still trying to please man, I would not be a servant of Christ."

I cannot please people a hundred percent of the time. That means failure will come—and when it does, I have to remember whose opinion matters.

When sinful human beings hurt you, it is wrong. Often, they should not be

When you think about how you have suffered, can you trust God to use that suffering not to destroy you but to save you?

doing whatever it is they are doing to you—but that doesn't mean that God isn't there using this very thing for glory.

Life to Joseph was the pits—literally. His brothers went from leaving him for dead in a deep hole, to selling him as a slave. Their hatred for him was sinful, but God used their sin for the good of others. If Joseph hadn't walked the road he walked, the nation of Israel wouldn't have survived.

Suffering often precedes salvation. When you think about how you have suffered, can you trust God to use that suffering not to destroy you but to save you? Can you see Him using your suffering as a flag of hope waving in the wind, drawing other sufferers your way and making you a signal to them that He can, and does, redeem the past for His glory?

It is my prayer that, if you have suffered at the hands of another, you would first let God comfort you with His grace and love. And that, when you have found that comfort, you will bless others with the same comfort you got from God.

I believe that when that happens—when you show and give comfort to others—all that you have gone through is not wasted but used as proof that God works all things together for the good of those who love Him.

10

I DON'T LIKE TO BOTHER PEOPLE

I don't like to bother people. I like to assume they are too busy to help me and go from there.

So rather than ask them for help, I just make a lot of noise in their direction until they volunteer to help. Like if the garbage is full and Michael doesn't seem to notice it, I'll say to the dogs, "No, don't get in that garbage. I know it's full, but stay out of it." Or if my daughter has left her shoes on the living room floor, I'll growl my disapproval and say something about having to "do all the work around here," as I reach down to put them away.

I don't like to impose on people and I resent that, so I make it known that I am peeved at them for *appearing* too busy to help me do what I never asked them to do.

I have mastered the art of assuming that nobody cares. So let me educate you in this overwhelming skill.

The first step is that you have to believe that your schedule takes priority over everyone else's. In other words, if *you* think it's time for something to be done, then, no matter what anyone else is doing, it *is* time for it to be done.

> *Knowing what others are thinking all the time is overwhelming!*

Second, you have to lay the foundation in your mind that because they haven't committed your plans to memory, they don't care about you.

Third, with this negative outlook firmly in hand, you can now presume that they will *never* help you, because if they were going to, they already would have.

Finally, you can begin the gentle and kind process of alerting them to their oversight while making some type of discontented sigh or side remark, until they finally see the error of their ways.

May you have better luck than I in this passive-aggressive but ever-so-sweet monologue of disgust. It has served me nothing but frustration, bitterness, and resentment for decades, and continues to be my instinctual invitation for intimate interactions—with myself. But I guess I'm just an optimist who believes the old adage that doing something over and over again while expecting a different outcome is the definition of *progress.*

Bet you wish we could be friends!

It's true though. I'm forever bemoaning how difficult it is to be so much more advanced than other people that I can assume their intentions and capacity for failing me very effortlessly.

I can walk into a room full of women and know before they do that they aren't going to notice or care about me. And I know this is just because of what they are thinking about me.

It's funny how discerning I am. In fact, an acquaintance of mine once said, "You just always seem so sad."

Well, you would be too if no one noticed or talked to you! Knowing what others are thinking all the time is overwhelming! And when I'm overwhelmed by their obvious disregard for me, I'm sad-faced, so sue me. I figure, "Why pretend to be happy when I know you're just going to make me sad?" I just cut out the middle woman that way.

Yes, the weeds growing in my overwhelmed garden are fertilized by the droppings of my imagination, as I assume things about others in order to prove their failure at doing what I want them to do.

U-G-L-Y!

Have you ever been to Chicago's Willis Tower (otherwise known as the Sears Tower) and stood on the glass-floored Skydeck? There you stand, four feet from the safety of the tower but nearly fourteen hundred feet from the place humans belong—on the ground. You are just hanging out, waiting for the floor to drop. Yeah, so enjoy that!

I bring up this sanity-defying feat because it's so analogous to how I often see myself in relationship to others.

The way I see it, on the Skydeck, I can look up or look down, but both views make me woozy. When I look up, I see people glaring down their noses, ready to disappoint; when I look down, I see the worst in others and compare it with my best.

My daddy told me what happens when I assume things about people: I'm always right and they're always wrong. And who wants to live with a bunch of people who are always wrong? So I've got to either change them or move out, and both options require a heck of a lot of work.

It's embarrassing. But when I expose the truth of my private thoughts this way, those things that I used to think made sense end up just being fodder for a stand-up comedy show. I mean, put your "reasoning" into writing and you start to see all kinds of laughable moments. But I'm telling you all this so that maybe you can see the absurdity in your own private monologue of misfortune and laugh with me.

THOUGHTS TO PONDER

I have figured out that whether I'm comparing myself to others or assuming they don't care for me, all of it is the same as worry: it's imagining things that I don't want to happen. Which wouldn't be a problem if people were just better at pleasing me; but alas, they are all too weak-minded and lazy to understand the value of *my* schedule and to-do lists. If only there were an answer!

Do people often fail you?

Do you feel like you spend more time taking care of things than being taken care of?

When people fail you, it hurts. It feels like they don't value you or your desires, and that can be overwhelming.

What do you do when people fail you?

When is the last time you resented someone for not thinking about your time or desires?

Do you often worry that things aren't being done that need to be done?

Assuming the worst in people destroys our ability to love and serve them, which is ironically what we deeply desire to do. It's like Paul says: "What I want to do I don't do, and what I do I hate." That's my life verse.

I want to be like Jesus; I want to take the failure of others as my cross to help bear, not my cross to burn.

But the more I acknowledge the sickness of comparing my goodness to your badness, or of assuming your bad thoughts about me, the more I am able to course-correct. It's like they say in those twelve-step programs—the first step is admitting you have a problem. Yay for first steps!

The truth is that, "We who are strong have an obligation to bear with the failings of the weak, and not to please ourselves" (Romans 15:1). We are meant to please others for their good, to build them up. Just like Christ, who didn't please Himself but took blame for the failures of others. I want to be like Jesus; I want to take the failure of others as my cross to help bear, not my cross to burn. I want to believe that I was made to bear with their failings, not to return them in kind.

And when I don't feel like I can do that, I want to remember the upside-down truth that "when I am weak, then I am strong" (2 Corinthians 12:10). I want to trust that, in those moments when all I want to do is complain, His grace is sufficient and His power made perfect in the very weakness I am feeling that moment.

III

WHAT I CAN'T CONTROL, CONTROLS ME

11

MY FACE JUST WON'T SHUT UP

My face just won't shut up—it's constantly commenting on the state of my soul, and it ain't pretty. I've even got the frown lines to prove it. Distrust, doubt, discontentment, disappointment, distress, and any other disturbance to my designs all push and pull my face around until it looks like a marionette caught in a tornado. And because of it, everyone who sees me knows exactly what I'm thinking before I get the chance to even decide if I want them to know. I'm powerless to the candor of my countenance, but at least it keeps me honest.

And honestly, I have a problem with control. I realize that I try to control situations not just because I'm bossy—that's only a means to an end—but because I have a deep need for comfort. And I am more comfortable if things get done my way rather than theirs. In fact, my optimal setting for life is comfort. All other settings start my face to flashing: "Emergency!

Check engine!" And from there, it's not long till I'm overheating and unable to go further.

I've actually taken stock and found that comfort informs all my life decisions and controls all my facial movements. I don't make a move without first determining if it would be comfortable or not. In fact, that's how I pick my words and fight my battles—is it a matter of comfort? Then my dukes are up.

So to my daughter who comes out of her room dressed like Punky Brewster, I say, "Are you sure you want to wear that? 'Cause that's embarrassing." OK, I might not say that, but my face sure does. Then I swallow hard and try to smile as I imagine what other women must be thinking of a mom with an eleven-year-old who wears a tutu over her jean shorts, with high-top sneakers, suspenders, and a crown.

Other moms' impressions of me deeply affect my comfort levels. Not living up to the crowd doesn't feel good at all. I desperately want to jump in and control the situation by rushing upstairs and putting together a more normal look for her, which she would hate. Instead, I bite my tongue and live to fight another day.

But it's not only family members that make me uncomfortable. Complete strangers do the same thing.

I'm attempting to let Him be God, though deep down I mistakenly feel like I could do it all better.

Before I became a pastor's wife, I used my vehicle like a teacher uses a ruler—to smack the hands of deficient students who don't follow the rules of the road. Tailgating, honking, passing quickly in the wrong lane—anything I could do to help my fellow drivers learn to drive more righter and to help me to get where I wanted quicker was fair game for me. Of course, after becoming a pastor's wife, I had to control my driving the way I'm now attempting to control my face. I'd stay a full car length behind the guy going 20 in a 35, and the one stopping in traffic to let someone turn in front of him out of a parking lot—because they just might know I'm a pastor's wife, and pastor's wives don't try to control other drivers. Or so I've been told.

Seriously, if anyone does something wrong (or not the way I would do it, in other words), I get the uncontrollable urge to fix it or, at the very least, to fix them so that they never do it again. It is literally uncomfortable for me when things are done in the wrong way, unless I'm the one doing it. And my definition of *wrong* is anything that makes me uncomfortable. Sit me at a table instead of a booth? Wrong! Bring me lime instead of lemon? Wrong! Interrupt me or make me late? Wrong! Wrong! Wrong! That's why I struggle with taking control, because people make my life miserable when I don't.

Doing whatever someone else wants me to do?

Eating whatever they bring me to eat?

Yuck!

And so I struggle not to tell the friend who is overbeating the muffin mix that it has to remain lumpy. And not to educate the one who leaves the skin on the cucumber that it's coated with wax. It's a struggle not to constantly teach everyone where they are going wrong. So, yeah, I'm a control freak, but a control freak in remission. At least that's my plan. I'm trying to suck it up and trust that God can talk to others as well as He can talk to me. I'm attempting to let Him be God, though deep down I mistakenly feel like I could do it all better.

THOUGHTS TO PONDER

Control is at the heart of the god complex that I struggle so frequently against. It's a condition suffered by millions of women across the globe, each of whom is sure that if everyone would just do what she told them, life would be so much better. But this god complex only ends up hurting everyone involved.

Plus, imagine how much more time you would have if you didn't have to manage the lives of everyone around you or worry about what they were constantly doing wrong. But comfort demands control. If you want the temperature to be comfortable, you need to control the thermostat. If you want people not to bother you, you have to exercise some control over situations that you assume they will put you through. And while it is good to have boundaries and not put yourself in harm's way, most of the time we use control not for safety but for our own pleasure. We complain, argue, admonish, and direct, so that ultimately we can achieve comfort.

Do you struggle with a need for comfort or is there something else at the root of your need for control?

What would happen if you didn't try to control the people in your life for the next twenty-four hours? Willing to give it a try?

How do you feel when other people attempt to control you?

How much of your overwhelmedness comes from not being able to control people enough?

Jesus knows the tendency of our hearts to want to pull the strings of life and control our worlds. He knows that we have dreams, plans, and hopes, and that they all revolve around our getting what we want. And that's at the heart of our overwhelming lives—we aren't getting what we think we need. So to the one who yearns for control, Jesus says, "Take care and be on your guard against all kinds of Godlike ambition, for one's life does not consist in being in control of everything" (Luke 12:15, Overwhelmed Woman version).

Can you believe that? That life isn't about you being in control of everything? If you can, then it's time to surrender—surrender your schedule, your comfort, and your plans to the One who knows even better than you what you need. As it says in Romans 12:1-2, "I appeal to you therefore, brothers, by the mercies of God, to present your bodies as a living sacrifice, holy and acceptable to God, which is your spiritual worship. Do not be conformed to this world, but be transformed by the renewal of your mind, that by testing you may discern what is the will of God, what is good and acceptable and perfect."

The world yearns to take control and encourages you to do the same, but as a child of God, you know who is ultimately in control. It is my prayer that you will trust Him today and no longer be conformed to this world.

12

I HAVE A PROBLEM WITH STUPID PEOPLE

God called Eve Adam's helpmate, and as a helpmate myself, I take my job seriously.

I help my husband drive.

I help my husband talk.

I help my husband dress.

I'm his little helper.

In fact, I don't know how he'd get anywhere if I weren't in the car telling him where to turn and when to slow down. If it weren't for me, I'm pretty sure he'd wear sweatpants and a dirty T-shirt every day of his life. He needs me—or, at least, that's what I think. He doesn't seem to agree, however.

He thinks he can do it all by himself—drive places, put on his clothes, finish a sentence. And that is why my life is so often overwhelmed. I don't understand why people can't just accept my control as not only inevitable but necessary. After all, four eyes are better than two, and what I'm really trying to

> *Whenever I'm not in control of a situation, I look for any opportunity to take control, simply because I know things are faster, safer, smarter, and more comfortable when I'm in charge.*

do is help. I mean, I wouldn't have to help him if he didn't miss perfectly good parking spots or look as if he were about to run over pedestrians. I wouldn't have to help him if he were more interested in dressing for success. Essentially, I wouldn't have to help him so much if he just did everything the way I think he should do it. Problem solved!

Or is it?

I know what to do, but I just can't seem to do it. And what I do, I hate. See, I know that he doesn't like it when I show him how much smarter I am than he is, and I know that "Let me help" is just another way to say, "You wanna fight?" So I try desperately not to "help" him, but it feels so counterintuitive that I can hardly hold my tongue. For example, while he's driving down the street talking, I often don't hear a word he says because I'm thinking, "Please take this next left! It's so much quicker than going straight." But I bite my tongue as he continues to talk so that by the time we get to the light I'm unable to hold it any longer. "Aren't you going to take Andrew Jackson Parkway?" I squeak out quickly, so as not to interrupt him for too long.

To which he says, "OK, so I guess it's more important to direct me than to listen to me. Have you learnt nothing?"

No, I haven't!

"Oh, no, I'm very interested in your story. I'm so sorry I interrupted you. Please go on." (Growth, apparently, means not always saying what you are thinking.)

I learned my lesson—kinda. So last week I tried a new sentence configuration to get him to do what I wanted without making him feel like he would be doing what I wanted.

The male brain is a very delicate thing. You must always figure out how to make a man think that what he is doing is his own idea. Otherwise, it's considered control—and for some odd reason, men don't like to be controlled. It's a flaw in their DNA, I think.

So I said, "I found out that turning here shaves five minutes off getting to the freeway." To which he grunted and said, "Ah." Then he continued on his merry straight way, leaving me to look longingly at the left-turn lane we *should* have been in.

The truth is that whenever I'm not in control of a situation, I look for any opportunity to take control, simply because I know things are faster, safer, smarter, and more comfortable when I'm in charge.

I guess you could say that I have a problem with stupid people, and my definition of *stupid* is anybody who doesn't agree with me or do things the way I do—because I'm pretty much always right. I've dedicated my life to it.

I never think that what I am doing and enjoying is wrong. If I thought it were wrong, I wouldn't be doing it. Or if, for some reason, I *were* doing what was wrong, I would be doing it only because I thought it was the right thing to do. Duh!

So since I'm making good choices, if you aren't doing it the way I am, you are doing it wrong. And because I love you and care about your choices, I need to correct you so that you

When we yearn for control, it is because we are discontent with how things are going.

75

know the right way to do it. That why I am constantly giving advice without being asked.

And this behavior isn't just unique to my role as wife. No, as a friend or enemy, I'm just as good at *helping*. It's the teacher in me—I'm dedicated to making everyone as smart as I am. Because when people don't do what I think they should, they are just plain stupid. It's the cross that I have to bear. [Insert sarcastic eye roll here.]

THOUGHTS TO PONDER

Apparently, I often think that being made the helper for a man means that I'm there to control all of his choices and actions. That's what *help* is—right? But I'm not sure that control can be considered help when all it does is hurt.

Even when I try to "help" my friends and family by telling them what to do, I'm aware enough to see that they aren't pleased to be bossed around, even if I'm sure I do know best.

In what ways do you try to "help" people by controlling them?

What is at the root of your "helping"? Is there anything selfish in the help? Anything controlling? If so, what?

Can you relate to my obsession with speed, safety, teaching, and comfort? If so, how do you act on that?

If you are not a controller, does your heart yearn for you to take control? If so, how does that affect your spirit?

The need for control is something that plagues a lot of us. When we aren't in control, life can feel out of control. But at the heart of our control issue is something spiritually destructive, and that is discontentment.

When we yearn for control, it is because we are discontent with how things are going. And this discontentment speaks more to who we think God is than to who we think others are. If we had true belief in the power and love of God, we wouldn't struggle so against our circumstances, because we would have learned the secret of being content in any situation, as the apostle Paul speaks of.

Discontentment keeps us on edge. It keeps us on the lookout for error and in constant conflict with the world around us. Even if we sit silently by, but are anxious on the inside, discontentment is still having its way with us.

On the other hand, when we sit back and trust that God can speak to the other person as easily as He can speak to us, and when we realize that our ways are not the only ways and that love sometimes lets others be wrong, then we can come to the conclusion that it won't mean the end of the world if we stay quiet; rather, it might mean just an extra five minutes to get there. A quiet heart is a joy to possess.

When we learn to live in the reality of the presence of God in all things, we no longer find ourselves playing god in the lives of others, directing their paths, determining their steps, and assuming that, without us, they would fall headlong into disaster.

It is only a sense of Godlike correctness that compels us to take control where no control is needed. But a soul that waits silently on the Lord finds relational relief. Psalm 62:1 says it best: "For God alone my soul waits in silence; from him comes my salvation."

13

A DIFFERENT KIND OF SELFISHNESS

If you need to know the negatives on a subject, give me a call. I'm an expert critical thinker—well, an expert criticizer, really.

Yeah, I'm good at that. I can find fault in almost anything or anyone. It's easy, really. I just look at all the things that I wouldn't do and don't like, and then think about them, and after just a second (I'm really fast!) it's like almost every word that falls out of my mouth is critical gold. It's that easy! I know, it's a gift. (Yep, sarcasm again.)

Though it just comes naturally to me, there was a time when I took that nature and perfected it. I mean I honed my craft. I studied. I practiced. I did my best to seek out all the bad in the world and criticize it. I found friends who had the same good sense as I did and got their *amens* as I pontificated on the pointless. It was exciting to be so enlightened that I could criticize without breaking a sweat.

> *Selfishness leads us to ignore God's Word, to hurt others, to overindulge, to be lazy, to steal, to kill, to fight, to manipulate, and to control.*

But then one day, I read these dreadful words in Romans 2:1-2, "Therefore you have no excuse, O man, every one of you who judges. For in passing judgment on another you condemn yourself, because you, the judge, practice the very same things. We know that the judgment of God rightly falls on those who practice such things."

Say what?

I scratched my brain and tried to see truth in the notion that I practiced the same things I desperately loved to judge. That couldn't be true; I would *never*! I didn't practice my selfishness the same way others did—I did it a totally different way!

Wait a minute. So it's just the manifestation of my selfishness that is different from everyone else's. In effect, when I'm criticizing you, I'm just criticizing your kind of selfishness while considering my kind of selfishness acceptable, and so I attempt to control you in order to save you from your kind of selfishness. What?

Hey, your kind of selfishness can be the exact kind of selfishness that I practice, and I'm still going to criticize you in order to control you. I figured this out when I actually listened to the words that were coming out of my mouth as I told my daughter that she was complaining too much. I told her I was tired of all of her whining about how her back hurt and how tired she was. How she didn't want to do anything but just lay down. I told her that complaining was a sin and that I wanted her to fight through the complaint and get to the joy by getting up and going, because I needed her to unload the dishes for me. As I walked off feeling good about teaching her a lesson, I suddenly tripped over the idea that I was just talking to little Hayley. My back hurts and I just want to sit down and take a load off eighty-five percent of the day. I complain about the weather, my aches and pains, my bad-hair days, and my lack of things to wear, and I'm criticizing her?

"Where did she get it?" I asked myself. "Eek! Monkey see, monkey do!"

I guess when you get right down to it, at the root of all the controlling desires in the world is that one terrible impulse of selfishness. That very thing that is the exact opposite of the most important thing God wants us all to have and do, which is to love. To love God with every ounce of our being and to love others as ourselves. Selfishness leads us to ignore God's Word, to hurt others, to overindulge, to be lazy, to steal, to kill, to fight, to manipulate, and to control. It all comes down to the opposite of love. And that is exactly what my criticism is—the opposite of love. For love is patient and kind, it's not all envious or boasting. It isn't arrogant or rude. It doesn't insist on its own kind of selfishness over another's. It isn't irritable or resentful because another's selfishness is a different kind of selfishness. It doesn't laugh when others get it wrong, but is happy with the truth. Love bears all things, believes all things, hopes all things, endures all things, and gives up control of most things. (1 Corinthians 13.)

> *We all have selfishness running through our flesh; it's the source of our sinful choices. But, as believers, we can reject selfishness in favor of love.*

81

When you think about it like that, it's kind of like agreeing with Oswald Chambers when he said, "In the spiritual domain nothing is accomplished by criticism."[1] Drat! And I thought I was saving the world by being so discerning and pointing out the error of everyone's ways. I thought I had a responsibility to be the watchdog, the corrector, the great critic, the fixer.

You know, sometimes growing in grace ruins all my fun.

NOTE

1. Oswald Chambers, "The Uncritical Temper," *My Utmost for His Highest* website, https://utmost.org/classic/the-uncritical-temper -classic/.

THOUGHTS TO PONDER

Criticism comes natural to the intelligent and the moral like myself. We all think we know how things should be done, so it's easy to insist that everyone else isn't as intelligent or moral as we are; however, criticism is really just another angle to get ourselves ahold of some control.

Do you ever find yourself criticizing others, if only in your thoughts? When?

Count your acts of selfishness. In what ways are you being selfish on a daily basis?

How do you use criticism to control others?

When we recognize our own selfishness, we gain the ability to love other selfish people, which means everyone. We all have selfishness running through our flesh; it's the source of our sinful choices. But, as believers, we can reject selfishness in favor of love. And love doesn't judge others for being just like we are, but offers them the same grace that we have accepted from our Savior for our selfishness.

That doesn't mean that we applaud the selfishness of others or make excuses for it; it just means that we don't use their selfishness as an excuse to control them or to make demands that they behave like we do, because we don't behave selflessly all the time either. Instead, in true selflessness, we can pray for those who fail us and attempt to restore in them a spirit of gentleness and understanding, having empathy for the humanity that makes them as selfish as it makes us.

Will you join me today in choosing grace over criticism? In letting God do the judging? Will you instead take up the mantle of love? And if you won't, don't worry—I won't criticize. You're safe with me.

14

I'M WHAT EXPERTS CALL WEIRD

Hi, my name is Hayley and I'm an interrupter.

Before you argue with me, let me tell you what I think you are going to say: "No you're not, Hayley. You'd never interrupt me."

Case in point: I just did.

You know why? Because I know what you are going to say before the words are on your tongue. I know them completely—that's why I don't need you to complete them. Most of my life, I have considered interrupting a communication skill in the category of active listening, and boy am I active. I'm like a sixty-pound puppy whose owner just got home—I'm

> *It's so hard when you first realize that you might not be as omniscient as you once thought.*

so interested in communication that I interrupt every step you take from the door to the couch. It's not that I'm *trying* to interrupt; I just can't seem to control my excitement. It's like I'm riding a wild mustang without reins, and she's all over the place!

The reason is twofold as I see it. I really do believe I know what you are about to say. That, combined with the fact that I don't have the patience to wait for you to say it, and suddenly you are unnecessary. I've got this conversation covered—just sit back and relax, and I'll take it from here. Yeah, that's at the root of my conversation confusion, and it's as frustrating to me as it is to you.

OK, maybe not. But it bothers me a little.

I do think there is a type of interrupter who interrupts just to switch the topic back to themselves, but that's really not me. I just want to cover as much ground as possible in this special time we have together. I'm what experts call weird.

I prefer quantity over quality.

For instance, the other day my PastorHoney (aka husband) had to start his sentence over three times because of my incorrect interruption insights. It went something like this:

> **PastorHoney:** So, the neighbor told me...
> **Hayley:** Oooh, that we could use his boat?
> **PastorHoney:** No, he said that he...
> **Hayley:** Oh, he's going to sell it, isn't he?
> **PastorHoney:** No, let me try this a third time.
> (That's the cue that interrupts my interruption.) The neighbor told me that he saw a groundhog in the yard.

What? How could I have gotten the conversation that wrong? You know, it makes me think that when I talk with people who don't know me as well as PastorHoney, I'm probably getting the conversation completely wrong when I speak for them. Ugh! How is that just now occurring to me? It's so hard when you first realize that you might not be as omniscient as you once thought.

> *To love people, we have to learn to listen, and listening involves the quietness of both mouth and spirit.*

What is it that the Bible says about my mouth? "Even a fool who keeps silent is considered wise; when he closes his lips, he is deemed intelligent" (Proverbs 17:28). Or in words that I can perhaps better understand, "Even an impatient woman who knows what you are going to say before you say it, but doesn't, is considered a good conversationalist; when she shuts up and listens, she doesn't look so ridiculous." Yeah, that hits me right on the head. Talk less, listen more, even if it takes them forever to get to the point.

THOUGHTS TO PONDER

Love lets them take all the time they need to say what they want to say. Love lets them talk about themselves without changing the subject to something more interesting. Love continues the conversational path that the loved one has chosen, instead of hurrying to change it to something about me.

To love people, we have to learn to listen, and listening involves the quietness of both mouth and spirit. You might have the closed-lip thing down while others are talking, but all the while your spirit is rehearsing what you will say next. If you can't listen with a quiet spirit, then you aren't really listening at all; you are only pretending to listen while you have a more important conversation with yourself.

How many times have you volleyed the conversational ball to your friend by telling her about something exciting in your life, only to have her drop your ball and toss you one that she chose instead? How disheartening is it when there isn't even as much as an acknowledgment of your feelings or experiences before the other person is off to the next subject? When someone attempts to control the conversation by refusing to volley your thought back to you, the feeling is as distasteful as a mouthful of mothballs.

In order to give up control, consider your conversational style. Are you an interrupter? If so, why do you interrupt?

How do you feel when you aren't in control of the conversation?

Would you say that you talk more than others, or less? In what way could you change that?

How does impatience factor into the interrupter's conversational style? Do you struggle with impatience? If so, how does that lead you to attempt to control others?

This week when you talk to people, try to keep the subject on them as long as you can by asking them questions and commenting on the things they say. Be encouraging and hopeful, and not critical. Love is selfless, which means we cannot love while being selfish. And conversations are the number one place where most of us practice selfishness.

In an attempt to love more deeply through conversation, many have opted to take one day a month when they do not speak. This practice of silence is a spiritual discipline that teaches us to rely on God to speak for us, to fight our battles, and to care for us. So many times, our conversations are all about self-protection, and we forget that God has that covered. Taking a retreat from talking for a day helps to remind you of that very thing.

IV

IT'S HARD BEING ME

15

"HUBBY, I HAVE A DATE WITH ANDREW TONIGHT"

In 2004, I wrote a best-selling book called *Mean Girls*.

So take *that*, mean girls who inspired it!

Yes, little did these girls know that the mean they showed me would be the source of my future income. But I can't give them all the credit. Let us go back to that time, shall we?

A time when I bravely decided to wear nothing but pink.

A time when the only place you would see my hair was up in two high pigtails.

A time when I believed that all girls were evil and out to get me.

A time when my best friends and constant companions were boys.

Yes, I was ripe for the picking.

The picking on.

What sane teenage girl could resist my low-hanging fruit of a life?

I was overwhelmed not only by memories of past hurts but also by the collision of my past with my present

Because I was shy (oh yeah, I forgot to mention that I didn't usually speak unless spoken to) and because I was five foot eleven with long legs and blonde curls, boys were my continual companions. That meant that I was earmarked as the most dangerous competitor my fellow predators could find. So I became the mean girls' victim of choice at my little high school.

The girls gave me a nickname to shame me. It was Bunny. It took me a while to understand why, but let me just say that Hugh Hefner would have been proud. When I started dating the quarterback of our football team, the girls decided to spray-paint the classy phrase, "Bunny-whipped" on his mom's driveway. I was famous. And what do people like to do to famous people? Threaten to kill them. The usual girlish pranks were soon topped by a vegan-friendly threat in the form of a carrot carved with a face, which I found hanging by a noose in my locker. Creepy, right?

Needless to say, the treatment I received at the hands of these little women was overwhelming. And in response to the overwhelming feeling of danger, I retreated further into the safe arms of the opposite sex. Boys don't scratch or claw, and they don't hiss or howl; they were less like cats and more like dogs. I know it's a cliché, but so was my life.

After high school, I continued to seek refuge with the male population and to fear the female of our species. While working for Nike corporate offices in Beaverton, Oregon, I found myself again the victim of mean girls who weren't my competition anymore, but my bosses. That made for a difficult season of life. Let's just say it fertilized and watered my dysfunctional fruit tree, and produced all kinds of isolation, bitterness, and self-protection.

And because I continued to see the mean side of women, I continued to isolate myself from them. I ended up married with only men as my best friends. This was not a good combo.

"Hey, Hubby, I have a date with Andrew tonight. Don't wait up!" That kind of arrangement wasn't received very well by Hubby, which, of course, totally blindsided me. I was oblivious to the condition of becoming a one-man woman.

So now, I was overwhelmed not only by memories of past hurts, but also by the collision of my past with my present—a collision in which only one male could survive. As difficult as our first year of marriage was, it could have been easier if I'd had a friend to talk to. But the mere topic of my friends was a huge source of our struggle, so I was left feeling alone in my overwhelmedness.

> *God picked a most otherworldly way to help me heal—by filling me with both the desire and the ability not only to forgive but also to love my enemies.*

It's taken me many years to build a stable of female friends—and it wasn't easy, I can tell you that. I just thank God that He allowed me to see how valuable girlfriends truly are. Now, I'm doing my best to learn to speak cat instead of dog.

THOUGHTS TO PONDER

Rejection, isolation, abuse—those things are life-altering. They give us scars that never quite go away. But, although my scars are sometimes very visible, I want to remember the scars that really matter: those of my Savior. Those are the marks that represent victory over death. It was His suffering that saved me, and it's my suffering that taught me more about Him. So I'm thankful for the wounds I experienced and happy to say He has healed them. And God picked a most otherworldly way to help me heal—by filling me with both the desire and the ability not only to forgive, but also to love, my enemies.

In what way have the actions of others overwhelmed your life?

Do you have any enemies? If so, how can you love them?

Are there people in your life that you are unwilling to forgive? If so, why?

If they asked you to forgive them today, could you? (Read Matthew 5:23-24 and Luke 17:3-4 to help you understand God's view on this topic.)

While speaking to throngs of wounded and broken people on a mount by the Sea of Galilee, Jesus offered us the ability to be free from the bondage of past abuse by saying:

> I say to you, Love your enemies and pray for
> those who persecute you, so that you may
> be sons of your Father who is in heaven. For

he makes his sun rise on the evil and on the good, and sends rain on the just and on the unjust. For if you love those who love you, what reward do you have? Do not even the tax collectors do the same? And if you greet only your brothers, what more are you doing than others? Do not even the Gentiles do the same? You therefore must be perfect, as your heavenly Father is perfect. (Matthew 5:44-48)

This view into what a life filled with the Spirit of God can do is refreshing. It means victory over the past, and a new pattern of love and forgiveness in the future. If you are suffering from what someone has said or done to you, you do not have to approve of what they did in order to pray for them or forgive them. You only have to rest assured of God's faithfulness and justice, and to trust that when you pray, you are set free—and that any power they had to overwhelm and control your life is gone.

16

I'M A CREEP LOOKING FOR A BFF

I do not have a best friend yet.

Let me tell you, you can't get one of those if you don't put your name on one by the end of school. High school preferably, but college is the drop-dead date for securing your own BFF. After that, they are all taken.

Friends are friends forever, or some junk like that. Even if they are separated by a long distance and are connected only through Instagram, Facebook, or texting, they're still able to remain locked at the hip.

It was ten years ago that I said good-bye to my last BFF and *his* name was Andrew, or Andy for short. So I started the BFF search decades too late. At first, I was a believer in finding my forever girlfriend. I can remember going to circle time with my two-year-old and scanning the crowd for my potential soul sister, like that one guy in the church singles' group who everyone avoids. At least that's how I felt. I'd smile at her, and she'd look down quickly and correct her baby. I'd scoot

> *We yearn to have our own tribe, to be a part of something bigger than ourselves.*

closer on the floor so our kids could become friends; I figured that might be a back door into the whole thing. But then they'd all just scoot away from the creepy lady.

I think we need to come up with mandatory BFF rings or something, so a girl knows if a woman is taken or not. It would save me a lot of heartache.

"Do you wanna have a playdate?"

"Who me? No, I'm spoken for. STACIE! LET'S GO GET LUNCH."

Drat, foiled again. If only I'd have known she was taken, I wouldn't have wasted all that time smelling her hair and complimenting her shoes.

Girls are hard to figure out. And so is it any wonder, with my past, that I have a hard time being optimistic about women friends?

But I don't want my past to define my future. If it did, I might be defined as a girl trying to be a boy trapped in a girl's body and hating everything girly but lovin' the boys. What a weird homeschool mom I'd be! So I'm allowing God to do what God does, and that is to make me a new creature: a woman in a woman's body, and happy to be here! It might take some time to fully recover from my past, but rather than letting it overwhelm me, I'm trying to see it as the fuel God uses to help me to speak to women like me—and to have compassion for the trials of everyone.

THOUGHTS TO PONDER

We were not made to be alone. We were made by a God who lives in community and wants us to live in community as well. When we don't have a solid community of believers who can lift us up when we get down and point us to truth when we start believing lies, it can be damaging to our hearts. We yearn to have our own tribe, to be a part of something bigger than ourselves. And we want that because that's how we were made.

Do you have a person who will point your eyes upward when you are feeling down?

What has God put you through in relationship to people that you can use to encourage others when they are feeling alone?

How might you contribute to or create a community of believers who love and serve one another?

What does God have to say about relationships in His Word?

I'm not so much overwhelmed with my past as with His ability to use it all for good. I want to be a sign to others who are hurting that the hurt doesn't have to be permanent. So when I am in a crowd, I look for the isolated girl, the lonely heart, to tell her she's not alone. I want to open up my circle to everyone and not show favoritism to one above another. Perhaps, that's why God hasn't given me a BFF; He knows I would shut myself up with her and never join in with those who are less fortunate. I do have a tendency to covet my own stuff.

But God, in His mercy, puts those who are strong into

difficult places, knowing that as they lift their hands like children asking their father to hold them, they will find strength in Him—a strength that will put theirs to shame and, in the process, allow them to minister to others who are now where they have been. Considering what God has allowed to happen in your life, who could you reach out to as a signal of what God can do for them?

17

I MAKE MY OWN LAW, THANK YOU VERY MUCH

As a do-it-yourselfer, I leave no job undone. I cut my own hair, make my own butter, write my own Bible studies, upcycle my own furniture, and make my own law, thank you very much. Considering myself a bit of an expert on, well, everything, I innately know that my way is the best way and, therefore, should be made into law. For example, my husband enjoys putting things off to the last minute. Doing them well in advance is sheer insanity to him, not to mention a royal waste of time that would be better spent playing video games (apparently). But "Thou shalt not procrastinate" is the first commandment of Hayley. I consider procrastinators sinners in need of my salvation, and so I do all I can to ensure they do whatever I ask them to at the very moment I ask them. And, no, that hasn't been a source of conflict between me and my husband—said me never!

Such a hater of procrastination am I that I determined at

> *When did I know I was overwhelmed by my own insanity? When obedience to God's law could only come after obedience to my own.*

a young age to do the exact opposite. (Isn't this how every smart person reacts to things they hate?) So whenever I received an assignment at school or work, I told myself I had to finish it in at least half the time I was given. I wanted to prove that I was better than everyone else who had three weeks to finish by getting it done in one and a half. Ha! Take that, you lazy lazersons.

This law that I created without even realizing it would then stress me out, because I was making myself do everything in not only half the time but also twice as well. Researchers have spotted similar behaviors in animals in the wild, and do you know what they call them? Dumb animals. That's me—I'm like a big dumb animal, stressing out over *not* the actual situation but one that I have invented in order to avoid being a procrastinator. I got brains and I'm not afraid to lose 'em.

Especially when it comes to my own laws. When I discovered that most of what was overwhelming me wasn't what I actually *had to do* but what I *told myself* I *needed to do*, either to look good, to be good, or to do good, I started to see the light at the end of my tunnel vision. And I saw that this self-imposed law was stressing me out because I wasn't equipped with enough energy, time, or money to do all that I demanded myself to do.

I can tell you I'm not alone in my insanity, however, because I've seen it in the lives of other women I know. There are a lot of us lawmakers out there, making laws and punishing those who break them, all in an effort to the get things done that need to be done. Using our own laws to make sense of life, to manage the chaos, and to direct the flow of traffic that is our world.

I unearthed one of those laws just recently when my daughter asked me if I could make her chicken nuggets for breakfast. I immediately said, "No, we don't eat chicken nuggets for breakfast. How about cereal, pancakes, or French toast?" She looked forlornly at me, and suddenly it hit me. Where is the Scripture that says, "Thou shalt not eat lunch for breakfast?" It wasn't God's Word but my own word I was enforcing, and so I quickly said, "What am I thinking? Of course you can have chicken. There's no law that says you can't!" Naturally, I want to feed her as healthfully as I can, what with her limited diet of chicken nuggets, mac and cheese, and hot dogs, but pretending like there is a law on *when* you can eat *what* you eat was just making life more of battle than it needed to be.

Over the years, I have identified a myriad of other such Capitol Hill–worthy bills that I have placed on myself, both subconsciously and deliberately, in an attempt to improve my life, avoid being hurt, or just git 'er done. And when I let those bills become law, I find myself overwhelmed by both my failure and the failure of others to do what I think must be done. For example, I used to think it was a requirement that the house be tidy and clean before anyone came through the front door. So, I wouldn't invite people over, because I didn't have time to set the stage for their grand entrance into my "perfectly kept" home. If I felt the uncontrollable compulsion to have them come, then I would sentence myself to eight hours of community service (aka housework) in order to fulfill the law of the tidy home, thus unknowingly putting my law above the godliness of hospitality. For me, cleanliness isn't next to godliness; it's across town and closed for repairs.

When did I know I was overwhelmed by my own insanity? When obedience to God's law could only come after obedience to my own law. When failure to fulfill my law ended in failure to fulfill His, I knew I had a problem.

THOUGHTS TO PONDER

If you are honest with yourself, you might find as I did that a lot of what overwhelms you is your self-imposed law. But the only law that ought to hem us in is God's law—and His law isn't overwhelming. In fact, His law is meant to produce the opposite fruit in our lives—the fruit of love and joy, peace and patience. When the only law we set as our standard is God's law, our to-do list loses a lot of its to-do's and to-don'ts.

You have created more to do than you were meant to do.

By way of example, doing the dishes can be an issue of self-control or of self-obsession. When you are overwhelmed with finishing the dishes, ask yourself, "Am I responding to God's commands or my own law in this emotional state?" The fact is, if you are obsessed with making sure there is never a dirty dish left in the sink when you go to bed, it is because of your own self-created law and order. God would prefer you to be peaceful and gentle, self-controlled, and content rather than stressed out and harried at the hands of your own laws.

What personal laws have you created in your life?

What emotional stress results when you fail to perform the way you tell yourself you are meant to perform?

Do any of your laws ever keep you from fulfilling God's law?

How much would it relieve your overwhelmed life to erase your law from the books and live only according to God's law?

The truth is, a lot of the relational problems we have find their root in our sense of responsibility to our own law. We resent others who don't keep our laws, or who reject or bad-mouth them. We fight to get everyone in line with how we think things should go when God determines how things should go. We stress when we don't do all that we have determined we must do, when it is God who works in us to do what we get done. A thorough assessment of your subconscious ideas of right and wrong, do's and don'ts, must-haves and can't-stands will reveal the areas in your life where you are overwhelmed. And it will show you that you are overwhelmed not because there is more to do than can be done, but because you have created more to do than you were meant to do.

This week, I hope that you can find peace and rest from your own personal law. Instead, meditate on the laws of God and especially on His grace, which is sufficient to cover all your failure, missteps, and misunderstandings. His grace takes away the law's power to punish and shame you and gives you back forgiveness, love, and mercy. What does your law give you when you fail at it? Will you choose today whom you will serve—yourself or your God?

18

WALK A MILE IN MY BRAIN

My mom would have made a great safety compliance officer for corporate America if she had worked away from home. She was the queen of instilling safety pointers and protecting me from the danger that is living. She loved ideas like these:

> Leave sooner, drive slower, live longer.
> Never give safety the day off.
> You're a sponge, and safety is the
> liquid; now soak it up.

With ideas like these firmly planted in my brain, I set off for college in the big city of Portland, Oregon, some four-and-a-half hours from my small hometown. I got a cute little studio apartment in an old 1940s hotel, which was conveniently located two blocks from campus. Happily, I would walk to school every morning and enjoy my time in the sun, but as soon as the sun was locked up for the night, sadly, so was I. From my fourth-floor window, I could see the darkness bleeding into the streets and invading the souls of the damned who circled the sidewalk in front of my building. At least that's how I imagined it. Even if I were completely out of food and starving to death, I would not leave the building after dark to trek the two blocks to the local grocer. It just didn't make good safety sense. *Remember, the safest risk is the one you don't take.*

Yeah, try walking a mile in my brain and see how you feel in the frightmare that is my life. My deep desire to explore the world and live the dream was overwhelmed by mere darkness—but boy, was it overwhelming.

Two years later, I moved to another apartment that was literally behind the grocery store. That way, I could open up my door and run as quickly as my little legs would carry me through the parking lot and into the safety of the Safeway.

Isn't it ironic? It really was called Safeway.

But the proximity of this store allowed me to take my first steps of emerging into the darkness. And like Dracula, when he first realized that the moon didn't burn like the sun, I was set free to live after six p.m.

My mind is easily drowned in fear, like a fly taking a swim in my lemonade, expecting the drink to be sweet but finding out it is deadly. Even so, I used to rely on my fear to protect me, "Do what it says and everything will be OK." In the vein of Dory from *Finding Nemo*, my chant was, "Just keep fearing, just keep fearing."

But fear isn't a loner.

> *I want to enjoy where my Father has put me and trust that He hasn't abandoned me. I want to rest and not fret, to trust and not fear.*

No, fear has a BFF that she pals around with, and her name is worry. In fact, some would say that worry is the one who gets fear all riled up in the first place, and I can attest to that. So many times in my life, worry has spoken and fear has reacted. I can say that I have successfully worried about thieves, fires, natural disasters, rabid dogs, living alone, dying alone, getting cancer, and being kidnapped, raped, and beaten. I've worried about just about everything a girl can worry about, and more. But let's be honest, the only success I had at such an endeavor was at giving myself an ulcer.

In my search for the cure, I read in a book that my worry was the result of my calling God a liar, and I didn't like that idea. So I set about finding out how to trust God rather than doubt Him. In order to do that, I had to know more about Him.

So I assigned myself the task of reading His Word and finding out who this God was whom I should trust. And as I read, it all started to make sense. If my mother loved me enough to try so hard to protect me, wouldn't my God do a much better job? Wouldn't He, too, want only what was best for me? This idea made a lot of sense, and over time it gave me a lot of freedom.

I still have to fight the urge to have my passport always ready, and the car full of gas in case I need to make a quick getaway like my mom always taught me. (I know, weird, but safety is no laughing matter!) But I try to remember the true story I read about a mom who left her daughter in the care of Hannah Whitall Smith, who said that all the girl did the entire time the mom was gone was fret and worry about her abandoning her. "She was too afraid to play, too scared to rest," said Hannah to the mother.[1] Imagine how grieved the mother was to hear that her child doubted her so and suffered so badly from it.

I don't want to waste my playtime on worry. I want to enjoy

THOUGHTS TO PONDER

Have you ever doubted God's protection?

Whenever we fear or worry, that's exactly what we do. We accuse Him of wrongdoing, and of lying when He says that if He is for us, none can be against us!

Did you get that? Is God for you? Then none, *nothing, no one, no matter how evil,* is against you. No one can separate you from the love of Christ, not *trouble or heartache or victimization or hunger or having nothing to wear or danger or a switchblade, nothing can pry His eyes and His heart from you.*

> *He doesn't walk away when we doubt Him; He's always right there waiting for us to come back.*

"No, in all these things we are more than conquerors through him who loved us. For I am sure that neither death nor life, nor angels nor rulers, nor things present nor things to come, nor powers, nor height nor depth, nor anything else in all creation, will be able to separate us from the love of God in Christ Jesus our Lord" (Romans 8:37-39).

That means that not the fear of death, or of demons, or of the past, or of the rich and powerful, of heights, or of ocean depths, or anything that God created, which is everything, can come between you and your God. Even if the very worst thing you could imagine were to come true, you would still be in His hands. Where is the room for worry, I ask myself.

How do you like to control your worry and fear?

Can you name two promises from the Word of God that ease your fear?

Imagine the worst thing you think could happen, and then imagine yourself telling God that it is OK as long as you have Him. Is that too much for you? Why or why not?

What do you believe that worry and fear accomplish?

It's hard being human. God knows it, and He has mercy on us. He doesn't walk away when we doubt Him; He's always right there waiting for us to come back. I am so thankful for that. Otherwise, I would have been lost a long time ago. But He has fresh mercy for this worn-out sinner.

19

THIS IS WHAT IT SOUNDS LIKE WHEN GRASS CRIES

'm not very good at suffering. In fact, if people got paid to suffer, I'd be broke, I do it so poorly. I'd be a sluggard just laying around watching my programs and eating bonbons. But I once met a woman who felt no pain. She could literally cut herself and not feel it. I was giddy when she told me about her condition.

"How amazing!" I said. "I want that condition!" I want to have the pain without feeling it. Then I'd be a dream to be around—no more complaining about my constant sore muscles, cold feet, or flu-like fatigue. No more suffering with discomfort. My dream come true. Yeah, being me ain't easy as long as I can feel.

The other day, my daughter and I were watching an educational video on how plants communicate. Yay, science!

And then the announcer told us that the smell of cut grass is the olfactory equivalent of a scream.

> *Maybe my DNA wasn't meant to influence my emotions as much as I had let it and that maybe it wouldn't be a lie to rejoice when all I wanted to do was complain.*

Screech! Say what?

Yes, that sweet scent that reminds us that summer is here is really the silent crying of thousands of tiny blades of grass being decapitated for our property perfection. Kinda makes you reconsider the compassion of being a vegetarian, doesn't it? I mean, people avoid meat so as not to have the shrieks of another living thing on their dietary conscience. I guess they didn't know that some shrieks are silent.

When I informed my husband of this fact, he stated, "Well, if everything suffers, we might as well start choosing our diet based on which cries are the most delicious."

My daughter then shrieked in delight, "Outback!"

I thank God that He didn't make it so that grass actually cries out in terror as the lawnmower growls to life, but gave us a sweet-scented return for our lawnicide. A smell so delicious that people have managed to bottle it and turn it into fragrances, candles, and cleaners. Ahh, the smell of death. What a gift.

If it were different, and the cries of our lawns could actually be heard, I'm certain that the green would overtake us, as we would do all we could to avoid the blood-curdling bellows that resulted from barbering our blades and trimming our turf. But thank God the opposite is true—that grass offers a gift as it gives up its life for our sense of order.

All this science made me wish I could be more like my

lawn, giving off my own spiritual version of cut grass every time I suffer. I imagined how it would be to make people sigh, not in frustration and disgust, but in peace and contentment, as I filled the air with the sweet scent of my suffering. Wouldn't that be something! But, alas, the opposite was true. When I grumbled, people's faces tightened and they braced themselves for the barrage of complaint. Perhaps, then, it wasn't a coincidence that my lawn was more weeds than grass, and the smell more oniony than sweet; this was obviously more analogous to my own response to being perfected by the Weedwackers of life. If I couldn't moan in agony, I could suffocate you with my noxious aroma. I got skills!

As I inhaled the toxic odor that is my failure at suffering, I began to regret the years of complaining conversations that I had started. I felt the loss of the wasted words of disgust and bitterness that had defined most of my close relationships, and I wanted a change. So I took a look into God's Word and this is what I found:

> We rejoice in our sufferings, knowing that
> suffering produces endurance, and endurance
> produces character, and character produces
> hope, and hope does not put us to shame,
> because God's love has been poured into our
> hearts through the Holy Spirit who has been
> given to us. (Romans 5:3-5)

All this time, I had thought that suffering was meant to produce fatigue, fear, and complaint. I literally felt, in the very center of my being, that to rejoice in my suffering, no matter how small, would be to lie to everyone around me—because the truth is, I'm not happy and I don't want to rejoice. But this passage made me think that maybe my DNA wasn't meant to influence my emotions as much as I had let it and that maybe it wouldn't be a lie to rejoice when all I wanted to do was complain.

Who knew that cut grass could send me onto the path of such great personal discovery and give us a picture of what rejoicing in suffering looks like? So now I pray that my (and your) response to suffering be like a best seller at Yankee Candle. Not for our glory, but for the glory of our God who loves us enough to prune us.

> *Making God's will more important than your own is the passageway from complaint to contentment.*

And as for my daughter's schoolwork, that gave us a nice, screaming salad.

Thanks, science!

THOUGHTS TO PONDER

Complaint is commonplace. You can hear it no matter where you go—in response to the weather, the wait, the service. We all naturally want to express what bothers us. But when we consider that God's plans for the difficulties in life aren't to plague us but to take us from despair to hope, that changes the honor we give to our complaints.

If your life produced a smell, what kind of smell would it be to the people around you?

On a daily basis, what do you find yourself most dissatisfied with?

What things are you thankful for in your life despite the discomfort they might bring?

If you had to choose between your will and God's will as it related to an important matter in your life—assuming the two were opposed to each other—which would you ultimately choose?

Making God's will more important to you than your own is the passageway from complaint to contentment. It's the secret sauce that gives those difficult situations in your life a taste of hope and a certainty that God's love is being poured into your heart. It's not always a sin to complain, but when we grumble against the things that God has allowed in our lives, we pollute our souls with the stench that results from accusing God of being absent and not doing the job we think He should. On the other hand, when we complain to God in the same way that the authors of the Psalms of Lament did, we bring our suffering to God trusting Him to protect and save us from the terror we see coming. (Read Psalm 74 to see what I mean.)

Our complaints aren't always fueled by tragedy; most often, they are fueled by our selfish desire to get what we want when we want it. The trouble with nurturing that kind of response in our souls is that it takes away our ability to love, since we cannot love others while we are selfishly consumed with our own lives. But when we allow the love of God to inform and inspire our love of others, we can begin to see beauty in even the most trying of situations. Trust that God hasn't left you or forsaken you, but that He is with you even in the moment of disquiet, in the time of trying. He will give you what you need to not only find hope in His salvation but also to rise above.

V

THE MISSION OF ME

20

MAYBE I SHOULD START KILLING PEOPLE

The "mission of me" is overwhelming.

This mission, chosen and designed by me, is to find comfort at all costs. Like a good missionary, I look for opportunities to fulfill this "great commission" in everything I do. From dealing with my family, friends, and even dogs to managing my work, travel, and sleep, it all has the undeniable undercurrent of my need to create unceasing serenity. I guess you could say that I have a comfortable worldview: if my world is comfortable, I'm happy.

When I'm living in pursuit of my mission, I'm living with the constant certainty that I will never get done what I want to get done because there just aren't enough hours in the day or enough people in the world to help me.

In fact, let's be honest, all people really do is get in my way. Maybe I should do what the Bible says and just start killing people. OK, maybe that's not what it says, but it should.

Of course it says the exact opposite: "Consider others more important than yourself." But that can't be right. I mean, I'm no Greek expert, but I am pretty discerning when it comes to the importance of others versus me. The idea that I should put others above myself is just plain dangerous—a threat to my mission—unless, ultimately, considering them more important somehow makes me more important. After all, it's got to be a win-win situation—at least according to my marketing-consultant brain.

All this makes sense to my heart, but as usual, my heart's a liar, spouting lies like Mrs. Liarson. What is it the Bible says? "The heart is deceitful above all things" (Jeremiah 17:9).

But why would my heart lie to me? It's me, and it only wants what's best for me.

And there it is: my heart only wants what's best for *me*. (Like I tell PastorHoney, "I always get there if I just talk long enough.")

And so my heart sets me out on the mission of me—to get all that I desire, dream, and have ever hoped for. Not that those things aren't good or even meant to be, but when I make them my mission instead of making God's mission my mission, I guess I make them my god, with a little *g*.

And "little g" just ain't no good.

"Little g" wants me to do more than I can so that I can have more than I have. And that is just laying the foundation for my overwhelming castle, where every room is a dungeon full of despair and dirty clothes. But when I trade my mission of me for

> *When you accept the mission of God and ditch the mission of me by the wayside, you walk from the darkness into that marvelous light!*

the mission of God, suddenly I'm not running the show, but He is. And it may sound surprising, but He's a lot better at this whole sovereignty thing than I am. Though I wish it were my superpower, it tragically never will be.

No, the most overwhelming events in my life have come while undertaking the mission of me. So I think it's time to give the controls for the mission over to One who's more highly qualified—and to begin training for the mission of the One who's qualified me to serve.

THOUGHTS TO PONDER

When you first received your "mission of me," you were but a child and the world was big and scary. You were only doing what survivalists call *surviving*. But as you grew, a more healthy and faithful mission was assigned you: the mission of God. And in this mission, God makes the plans, sets the course, and decides good from bad. As the Bible says, "You are a chosen race, a royal priesthood, a holy nation, a people for his own possession, that you may proclaim the excellencies of him who called you out of darkness into his marvelous light" (1 Peter 2:9).

When you accept the mission of God and ditch the mission of me by the wayside, you walk from the darkness into that marvelous light! And the beautiful thing about light is that it keeps you from doing stupid things like stubbing your toe or falling for a tyrant. When the light is on, you can see what or who is in front of you.

John Piper said something similar to this when he told the tale of a woman who was locked in a dark room. She could feel something warm, soft, and furry with her right hand, and something that had a cold, sharp edge with the other. So her natural instinct was to draw closer to the soft and furry. But when the light went on, she was able to see that the warm, soft fur belonged to the underbelly of a horrid, man-eating monster; and the hard, cold edge was the sword of the majestic Christ ready to save her. The reason she had gravitated to the monster was that she was in the dark.[1]

Everyone who lives for the mission of me lives in the dark, and in the dark we fall for all kinds of lies.

But if you are living in the dark, you can choose to get out of it. And the first step is to give up the mission of me in favor of the mission of God. That means that His will for you will always upstage your own. You will want whatever

He wants for you, even at the expense of your hopes and dreams.

What are some mission of me dreams (like my search for comfort) that you are unwilling to give up just yet?

Do those unfulfilled dreams torment you or keep you overwhelmed?

How would thinking of your life as a mission for God change your everyday routine?

Is there one area where, if you are honest, you would be hard-pressed to choose God's will in, if it contradicted your own? Pray for the strength today to be able to accept His will with joy.

The mission of God might seem like a mission impossible, but it's only impossible if He's not the one who makes it happen. The real mission impossible is the mission of me. Finding satisfaction, hope, comfort, love, joy, and everything I dream of is impossible when I do it for myself. And it's the same for you.

When I first gave thought to the difference between these two missions, I immediately saw the beauty of giving up my own, and desperately wanted to be done with it. I won't say that I have converted to His will a hundred percent of the time, but I can say that the more I think on the mission of God, the more I can see the events in my life with clarity, faith, and hope—no matter how much they might contradict the mission of me.

God's mission has to do with one thing and one thing only. Love.

Note

1. John Piper, "Let Us Walk in the Light of God," Desiring God website, February 3, 1985, www.desiringgod.org/messages/let-us-walk-in-the -light-of-god.

21

ENLARGING MY GOITER

I've spent a long time thinking that finishing my to-do list was somehow furthering God's kingdom, checkmark by checkmark. I mean, I'm a book-writing homeschool mom: I have a house to clean, meals to cook, books to write, talks to prepare.

Obviously, doing all of those things should be the focus of my life, since those are my jobs. But those jobs are exhausting my adrenals and enlarging my goiter. In an alternate universe, where God's mission replaces mine, would my goiter be less engorged and my fruit less rotten? Because I've got lots of rotten fruit: between the stress and frustration, there's a whole orchard floor of rotten!

When I wake up in the morning and create my to-do list, I most often have *my* mission in mind. I'm thinking about all that will make my day go smoother: doing the dishes, sweeping the floor, making the beds. I want to organize and sort. I want to get things written and make deadlines. But I've noticed that my mission isn't always God's mission. And

I can say that with authority because of all the interruption. "What kind of authority is interruption?" you ask astutely. Well, thanks for being so astute.

The Bible calls God sovereign, meaning that nothing happens unless He allows it to happen. He says, "I am God, and there is no other; I am God, and there is none like me, declaring the end from the beginning and from ancient times things not yet done, saying, 'My counsel shall stand, and I will accomplish all my purpose'" (Isaiah 46:9-10).

"Who has spoken and it came to pass, unless the Lord has commanded it? Is it not from the mouth of the Most High that good and bad come?" (Lamentations 3:37-38)

So, let me ask you, who will interrupt you unless the Lord has allowed it? God is omnipotent, so the question begs to be asked: did God allow the interruption to my schedule, even the "bad" interruption, to come to pass?

Can you believe that the fruit of the Spirit finds fertile ground in moments of interruption? In other words, that it grows most when it's needed most? You don't need the fruit of love, joy, peace, patience, kindness, goodness, faithfulness, gentleness, or self-control when there is no one around to bother or frustrate you. No, those things come naturally when it's all kittens and candy. But when someone interrupts your mission, when they ask you to end your efficiency, that's when it ain't nothin' but a fruit of the Spirit thang. You need God to give you evidence that He lives in you in those moments when other people are messing with your mission.

> God's mission is never interrupted and is always completed; it's just not always completed in the ways we might expect.

When we are so focused on the mission of me, we miss the opportunity to participate in the mission of God. His mission has very little to do with organization and cleaning, with deadlines and financial freedom. His mission has to do with one thing and one thing only. Do you know what that is?

The Pharisees wondered this very thing, when they asked Jesus, "Which is the great commandment in the Law?" His answer forms the foundation of His mission for us on earth, and the answer wasn't to get things organized, to git 'er done, or to finish what you've started. Nope, His mission was love. And He gave that mission to us in Matthew 22:36-40: "Love the Lord your God with all your heart and with all your soul and with all your mind." And, "Love your neighbor as yourself."

The mission of me will forever be in the crosshairs of the world—to slow you down, derail you, and otherwise tick you off. But when you move from the mission of me to the mission of God, no matter what the derailment might be, you can know you are still on mission. And when your mission is to love, that means that your to-do list is going to take a beatin'. Believe me, I know. In fact, I have to stop writing at this exact moment because my daughter, who is working at our church, wants me (instead of her dad) to come pick her up. She misses me because I've been working so much. But! I'm on a roll here! So I really don't want to leave. This roll stuff doesn't happen all the time.

But after thinking about what I'm preaching here, I have decided to go get her. Ugh! Interruption! But all the way there, I will be trying to remember whose mission I'm on and who controls the time I have to achieve it.

So, here goes. What you read next will be written when I get back!

OK, well that was sweet. Glad I went to her when she called.

Listen, I don't know if my first response to interruption will ever be joy, but I am praying that it will be eventually. I tell my husband that I am a slow adopter. I don't like new car-body styles; I like the old ones. I don't jump at the chance to have my schedule changed; I like "practice makes perfect." So earlier, it took me like five minutes to respond to my daughter's text, because I wanted to stay, but I felt I should go. Conflict! Argh!

I'm not perfect, obviously, but I do want to imitate the perfect One, and so I want to say to the Martha inside me what Jesus said to His Martha: "Stop doing the dishes and get out here and love." (Luke 10: 38-42.) I want to allow Jesus to interrupt my plans and to keep me on His mission instead of enslaved to my own.

THOUGHTS TO PONDER

How do you deal with interruption?
If you think about those interruptions or derailments as coming from God, how would that affect your day differently?

The mission of me is overwhelming because it is forever being interrupted. But the mission of God is never wrongly interrupted.

Can you exchange your mission for God's?

What is one thing you could do to start that transition?

Looking back at your life, what bad things have happened that God has used for good?

Here's a thought: if God always gets what He wants, and I want whatever He wants, wouldn't it stand to reason that I would always get what I want? Philosophy!

That's the amazingly freeing thing about being on mission for God over self. When you are on God's mission, you always get what you want because you want whatever He wants—and being sovereign, what He wants is exactly what He gets. That just means that every interruption or trial, everything that happens to you, will work together for your good. When you are certain of that, and certain that His mission is the only mission you were made for, then you can be set free to live life unencumbered by interruptions and unfinished to-do lists. God's mission is never interrupted and is always completed; it's just not always completed in the ways we might expect.

22

THE GLASS IS HALF FULL (OF TOXINS)

Not to beat a dead horse, but my natural tendency is to assume the worst. It's not that I see the glass as half empty; I just see it half full with toxic chemicals that are tasteless and odorless and slowly killing me and my family. I'm not a pessimist. I'm just good at doing my research, so I know exactly how dangerous this world has become.

I'm pretty sure that danger is a more probable outcome than safety in just about every situation. The worst-case scenario just rings more true to my educated mind.

You see, I know things.

So, when they told me about Y2K, I knew it was true. How could the computers keep going with all those zeros? Obviously, everything was going to stop working on January 1, 2000, and chaos would come next. So, I began to stock up on the necessities: water, canned foods, thermal blankets.

I put more deadbolts on the door in case of zombies.

I wasn't going into this new world unprepared.

It might not surprise you, but I border on—what's the word? *Hypochondria*. That's it.

But I just border on it. As you know, I don't like to fully commit to anything. I do suffer from really bad headaches though, or what I like to call *brain cancer*. And I have this constant pain in my gut after I eat: *colon cancer*.

I mean the doctor says it's not colon cancer, but she's the one just "practicing," so what does she know? I'm the one livin' it!

That's why I changed primary care physicians. Now I'm serviced by Dr. Google. He gets me. And working with him is so easy! All I have to do is type my symptoms into the search bar, and in less than two seconds he gives me 101 terrible things that could be wrong with me. It's a smorgasbord of suffering, and I'm an overeater!

Understandably, I prefer to pick the worst possible option. People who don't really care about their bodies settle on the simplest answer, but I've got high standards for how I care for myself. I want to be free from this pain and suffering, so I'm not settling on a cold if there is the option for meningitis. Give me meningitis every time—at least that will explain why I feel so awful.

But because I take such good care of my body, I then also look for the least invasive treatment I can find. So I type in "natural healing for colon cancer."

Nine times out of ten, when you type in "natural healing," the first result is garlic: it kills everything. Then I add in some essential oils, and maybe a little castor oil. I'm totally retro in my healing. OK, maybe not retro; maybe more like medieval. I like things that have stood the test of time. I mean, *garlic*— that's been working since the time of Dracula, and all those peasants with pitchforks just can't be wrong.

But seriously, the plethora of illnesses out there does tend to overwhelm me. My daughter, Addy, had three little bumps on her leg last night. They looked like small water blisters, and you might have thought

> *I'm overwhelmed with the imaginary over the factual, and the future over the present.*

they were bug bites if you weren't as discerning as I am. But because they were in the form of a perfect triangle, my early alert system went off.

"This is so unusual. It's got to be disastrous," I figured.

You know how God designed the poisonous creatures of the Amazon to be brightly colored so as to warn us to not mess with them? I figure He also designed a perfect triangle of blisters to alert me to implement panic mode. So I went to Dr. Google for a quick diagnosis.

My heart sank as I saw images of kids covered in blisters, bug bites that had festered into three-inch craters, and parasites that leave rings all over your skin. I mean, this world is a sick place and I'm living in it. The sheer amount of potential answers to my inquiry filled me with dread.

But I talked to Michael, and he said to "put some itch cream on it" and put her to sleep.

So I did.

The next morning, I asked her how it was, and she said it was gone!

Gone!

Can you imagine that?

I was so stressed about this unknown disease, and it was gone in less than fourteen hours.

I think if I could go back and calculate all the overwhelming things in my life, I'd find out that I've been more overwhelmed by things that never happened than by things that did.

In fact, it seems that when the things that are *actually* happening are *really* bad, I'm far better at managing my stress than when I am *imagining* things that are highly unlikely. At least when things are happening, I know with certainty what I'm dealing with.

> *I have noticed that whatever it is that is overwhelming me most often points to my mission.*

I know that God said He won't give us more than we can *bear*. So I have to remember that all this stuff I can't seem to *bear* isn't His breaking His promises to me, but is only my imagining *bears* that turn out to be bunnies. That means I'm overwhelmed with the imaginary over the factual, and the future over the present. I am not considering that, when He says He won't give me more than I can bear, He means that He won't give me more than I can bear while abiding in His grace.

If I'm overwhelmed, it's because I'm not resting in the knowledge that I'm made for His mission and not my own. When I'm on His mission, He is set on seeing me through and perfecting me. Otherwise, 2 Corinthians 9:8 wouldn't be true: "And God is able to make all grace abound to you, so that having all sufficiency in all things at all times, you may abound in every good work."

THOUGHTS TO PONDER

What is your mission in life? If you look at everything you do—all the things that overwhelm you—and ask yourself why you do them, what would you say is your ultimate reason? What is your mission? To be happy? To be a good mom, a good wife, a good friend? Is your mission to move up in the world financially, positionally, or spiritually?

I have noticed that whatever it is that is overwhelming me most often points to my mission. So when I start to become overwhelmed by the sheer amount of stuff I have lying undone before me, I ask myself what my life's mission is and how this list, this emotion, or this state of mind serves that mission.

What is your mission in life? Why do you do what you do all day long?

What happens when you don't succeed at your mission? Do you feel overwhelmed?

How does this mission line up with God's mission?

What is God's mission for your life?

God's mission, according to Jesus, is to, "Go therefore and make disciples of all nations, baptizing them in the name of the Father and of the Son and of the Holy Spirit, teaching them to observe all that I have commanded you" (Matthew 28:19-20).

God's mission is always to further His kingdom, but my mission often ends up being dictated by what I like to call my "needs." My needs for comfort, control, and contentment—those are my big three. Looking at my to-do list from time to time, however, takes my temperature on how well I'm serving

God's mission over my own. I usually realize that none of the items on my list of "needs" are on His list. Though while serving His mission, I might be able to cross off a few items on my own list, but getting them done as a symptom of serving Him is far more rewarding and faithful than making them the mission of my life.

Humanity has been cursed with the mission of me since the time of the fall, and that mission has built massive civilizations, raised enormous structures, and created billions in wealth, but those things will eventually all pass away.

What is your mission in life? Do you have just one, or can you list a few?

Discover your mission today by praying and thinking about what God has planned for you as a keeper of His Spirit and His Word. When you make your mission the same as His, you know that your mission will never be thwarted, interrupted, or destroyed, but that everything—including every delay and every roadblock—is part and parcel of His mission for you.

23

DEEP UNDERCOVER IN MUMBAI

What do hypochondria and international espionage have in common?

Me, that's what.

How a girl who is constantly sure the worst will happen could have ever dreamt of going into covert operations for the U.S. government is beyond me. Maybe it had something to do with putting all of my skill sets to work in one career. What else would an actress who specialized in foreign languages and studied political science do for a living? It was the perfect cocktail for my much-dreamt-about stint at "The Farm," working for "The Company," and planning my exfils and infils. See, I speak spy!

Anyway, during my years of theater training, I was looking for someone to help me with my CIA prep, so I found a girl on campus who told me about a guy who was on the same track.

I went to see him.

He was in the theater building running some kind of audition, so I snuck in quietly and sat down in an empty seat. After about three minutes, he said, "You! Get up there!" He pointed to me and then the stage. I shook my head and hesitantly stood, attempting to tell him, without making a scene, that I wasn't there to audition. He wasn't interested in my stories, so his assistant hurried me onto stage and said, "Good luck!"

In the first scene, the director—my CIA guy—called out a situation and a character that I had to improvise. I got "East Indian" as my character. I can't remember the situation now, but I vividly remember doing my much-practiced East Indian male impersonation (much-practiced because you never know when the Norwegian girl will be sent deep undercover into Mumbai). But apparently I had mastered the tradecraft, because I had them all in stitches. Before I knew it, I was a member of the cast of 60 Toes, Southern Oregon State College's premier improv troop.

> Can I trust God with my schedule and be willing to miss out on something I wanted to do?

The thing I love about improv is that it doesn't require loyalty to a script; it's more organic than that, like the spy biz. When you love improv, you love flying by the seat of your pants, going with the flow, doing whatever seems to come next. Naturally, there's nothing planned and plotted out, so it's great for commitment-phobes like me.

Whether it comes from my love of improv or my broken family, I am easily overwhelmed by commitment. Where other women have to have playdates and lunches scheduled two weeks in advance, I prefer an open social calendar with room to jump between two speeding boats or repel from tall buildings, all in an attempt to get away without getting caught.

Yes, the more commitments on my calendar, the sicker to my stomach I get. When I have an appointment looming, my nerves are on end and my anxiety doubles. I can't seem to do anything other than wait to leave in enough time to arrive five minutes early, just so I won't be late.

I know, I'm a freak.

I've had neuroses that have their own neuroses.

Maybe I would have done better to have followed in Woody Allen's footsteps rather than Austin Powers'.

At the root of my fear of relational commitment, though, is my whole worst-case-scenario training. I assume that any commitment I make can, and probably will, be trumped by a much better opportunity between now and then. Which just speaks to my desire to control the world, à la Mr. Evil and his kitty Mr. Bigglesworth. Or, in more spiritual terms, it speaks to my inability to trust God with my schedule and to simply grow wherever I'm planted—or sent.

So I'm going to try and make a few commitments this week, not because I want to control my schedule, but because I want to kill my phobia and trust God with the things that most run against the grain of my life. I'll just roll the dice and hope for the best.

And, wait!

I think I'll also consider Proverbs 16:33 my daily planner verse: "The lot is cast into the lap, but its every decision is from the LORD."

It might be a game of chance, what happens tomorrow or next week, but God owns the house, so I'm gonna trust Him with it all. If I'm scared to do it, or it freaks me out just thinking about it, then I'll remind myself that it's better to dive in and see the depths where God wants to take me than to remain in the shallows, afraid of the sharks.

Forever, my spiritual excuse for not committing to too much has been to say that if the Lord wills it, I will do it, and if not, then I won't. But why can't that just as well apply to planned activities? I can make plans and then trust that if God wants them to happen, He'll make things go as planned; and if He doesn't, He will make sure that something else gets in the way. Trusting Him is really the thing. Can I trust God with my schedule and be willing to miss out on something I wanted to do? Or be joyful when He changes plans that I was really excited about? That is my prayer. Now may our God and Father himself, and our Lord Jesus, direct my way in all that I do.

THOUGHTS TO PONDER

Not everyone is commitment-phobic, I know. I have friends who will not do anything with me in the spur of the moment, insisting I get on their calendar, or their lives will fall apart. It's as if their calendar has to give me approval before they will consider me worthy. So I know not everyone is mixed up like I am. But they *are* mixed up; we all are. It's because we are human.

The amazing thing about being a human saved by grace is that God never leaves you the way you are. He is constantly changing His children. He is always growing us and showing us the parts of our lives that are standing in between Him and us. The only difference is that some of us love change, and some of us are scared to death of it.

How do you feel about change?

What is God wanting to change in you today? Spend some time thinking and praying about it.

What is one thing that you could do today to show God that your mission is debunked and you are giving up your own plans for His?

Consider God's sovereignty today. Meditate on it. Study it, make it known to your soul, and rest in it.

God wants us to grow. If we aren't growing, we are dying. And the believer is brought into life and out of death. In Romans 12:2,

God never asks the impossible without giving us the power to do it.

Paul encourages us not to be "conformed to this world, but be transformed by the renewal of your mind, that by testing you may discern what is the will of God, what is good and acceptable and perfect."

The world is our home—we were raised in it and live in it daily. Not being conformed to it is like asking a fish not to use its gills. But God never asks the impossible without giving us the power to do it. Through His Holy Spirit, we were made new creatures. Not only that, but—as we see in Colossians 3:10—we are continuing to be renewed in knowledge, after the image of our Creator. That means that every day, we are growing and becoming more like Christ, which says that change must become our friend. The believer covets change because, without change, we are simply resisting being drawn closer to Christ.

I pray that change will be your friend and your mission, as it is the mission of God for all believers. And with His mission always comes the promise that He will do for us what we cannot do ourselves.

"For it is God who works in you, both to will and to work for his good pleasure" (Philippians 2:13).

24

GOD'S TO-DO-THROUGH-YOU LIST

Confession time.

One time—OK, maybe two—I got mad at my nine-year-old because she didn't want to pray before bed. I was trying to teach her about a life of faith, but she wasn't interested, and that just ticked me off. So I mocked her, told her I was done putting her to bed, and stormed out of the room. *Take that, you little heathen! Maybe next time you'll have the decency to glorify God and pray with me! Grrr!*

More times than I care to mention, I've been late for church and got stuck behind people going ten miles under the speed limit. So I tailgated them until they finally got out of my way, and then sped past them in disgust.

Repeatedly, I've had projects due and been so overwhelmed with their size and my lack of time that I stressed myself into inaction. I literally didn't know where to start and so I didn't. In one instance, worry got the better of me and made me too stressed to write my Bible study about the fruit of the Spirit. Ironic?

Do I need to go on or do you get the picture? I have a plan of action—a to-do list—and somehow it goes all wrong. This is usually someone else's fault—someone who is thwarting my plans and getting in my way—and this demands action on my part. Too many times to count, that action (or reaction) has been anger, frustration, resentment, and stress. In fact, when things don't go my way, that's pretty much my natural response one hundred percent of the time. Like, say I can't get a knob to turn on an appliance. I might just put a little extra force into it out of spite, prove to it who's boss, and end up breaking the thing in irrational retaliation. Not that I would ever tell my husband that.

As I've said before, and to restate the apostle Paul's confession found in Romans 7–8, what I want to do (be faithful) I do not do, but what I do (retaliate) I hate. And if I do what I do not want to do (stress out), I agree that the law (don't be anxious about anything) is good. As it is, it is no longer I myself who do it (so don't get mad at me), but it is sin living in me (because of my parents). For I know that good itself (perfection) does not dwell in me, that is, in my sinful nature (I'm only human).

For I have the desire to do what is good (be the best), but I cannot carry it out (because of you). For I do not do the good I want to do (be patient and kind), but the evil I do not want to do (act on my anger)—this I keep on doing (because it feels good).

Now if I do what I do not want to do (act like a heathen), it is no longer I who do it (so get off my back), but it is sin living in me that does it (hate the sin, not the sinner).

So I find this law at work: Although I want to do good (produce the fruit of the Spirit), evil is right there with me (my flesh). For in my inner being I delight in God's law (I'm an angel); but I see another law at work in me (and I don't like breaking the law), waging war against the law

What's on His list? It's simple, really. Just one thing: love.

of my mind and making me a prisoner of the law of sin at work within me (free Hayley!).

What a wretched woman I am! Who will rescue me from this body that is subject to death?

Thanks be to God, who delivers me through Jesus Christ our Lord! Therefore, there is now no condemnation for those who are in Christ Jesus, because through Christ Jesus the law of the Spirit who gives life has set you free from the law of sin and death. (See Romans 7–8:1.)

So in my attempt to be faithful, to teach my child about God, to go to church regularly, and to write my Christian books, I've managed to use sin as my method of regaining control.

Nice. Way to go, Hayley! Way to make what you want to do more important than what God wants you to do!

THOUGHTS TO PONDER

Can you relate? Have you ever looked at your day and said, "Well, that was a big fail!" I think that if you are honest, you will say yes. When the to-do list doesn't do what it's supposed to do, it's easy to get so overwhelmed that faithfulness, and all that goes with it, is gone. You know that's not how things are supposed to go, but you feel powerless to change it.

Can you recall a time when you blew your witness with your overwhelming emotions?

What is your normal reaction to interruption, failure, rejection, and inconvenience?

Which of these reactions do you consider acceptable when things don't go the way you want them to go?

Anger

Frustration

Bitterness

Resentment

Gluttony

Sadness

Impatience

Harshness

Argumentativeness

The truth is that most of us fall back on these reactions when we get overwhelmed by life. They promise to get things done and get things moving, so we accept them to stop the overwhelming feeling of being out of control. In the end, we know that's not how we want to live, but we often just can't find a way out. And that remains the case as long as we live by our to-do lists instead of by God's to-do-through-you list.

What's on His list? It's simple, really. Just one thing: love.

All God has for you today, and every day, is to love. That's the sum of all of His commands: love Him with everything and love your neighbor as yourself. If you do that, you've done all that He has asked you to do.

But how do you do that when you have a list of your own that has to get done? That's a good question. The answer is this: if you can't do something on your list in love, then it's time to surrender the mission of me to the mission of God. That means if there is something you cannot do in love, either delete it from your list or ask God to help you do it lovingly with the power of His Holy Spirit. That is the only way that you can truly love difficult, trying, and stubborn people in troubling, challenging, and hopeless situations—through His Holy Spirit.

If you wake up tomorrow dead-set on the mission of God, resolved that love is the Instagram filter of your life, and determined that you won't do anything without love being job number one, then tomorrow will be less overwhelming than today. And if you keep God's mission as your goal for the rest of your life, you will find yourself less overwhelmed by life and more overwhelmed by your God.

When love takes priority, God gets the glory. And what gets done may not necessarily be what you had in mind, but it will ultimately give God glory, as you go about His mission over your own.

VI

OVERWHELMED BY GOD

<u>25</u>

GO OVERWHELMED OR GO HOME

few months ago, I started watching *Downton Abbey.*
I know, what took me so long, right?
I'd heard all the talk about how great it was, but I
don't like bandwagons—they are too loud and crowded. So,
I took my own sweet time.
Once I started watching,
though, I was hooked. I

> *When I love something,
> most of my thoughts and
> words are devoted to it.*

watched the entire six seasons in two months, and
I loved it! In fact, I loved it
so much I was desperate to
talk about it. But of course, everyone else had watched it years
before, so there was no one to talk about it with.

My only alternative was to think about it. Constantly.
That's what happens when you overdose on something good.

I used to find myself overwhelmed with thinking about the

characters as if they were a part of my family. *Why doesn't Anna just tell Bates about the rape?* I'd work over answers to their problems for ten minutes before I even realized what I was doing. It consumed me. I even dreamed about them at night.

When I love something, most of my thoughts and words are devoted to it. I give whatever gives me the most joy all the glory, because my joy yearns to find a voice; it wants to be heard and shared with others. It's almost like talking about it makes my joy complete.

In the same vein, when I find something good for me, I figure it will be good for everyone who is like me—which I assume is everyone. (Sometimes I mistakenly categorize myself as normal, but life soon educates me otherwise.) So, when I was young and single, I decided what any normal girl just out of college would, and I started my own Mary Kay business. I mean, who doesn't want to be her own boss and set her own hours, all the while making the future look beautiful? Another consultant who lived in my apartment complex had told me I could become independently wealthy if I just joined her team. I was in! Who cares if she lived in the same dumpy apartment building as I did? We were on our way to financial independence together!

All I had to do was to pay for my initial starter kit, then it would be raining money through the sunroof of my pink Cadillac. But it wasn't just the idea of all that money that inspired me—or so I tell myself—it was the product itself. I was a true believer. I had always had bad skin, but when I put on the Mary Kay product, my face went from gravel road to baby's butt in sixty seconds.

As soon as my kit of independence arrived, it was makeup on! Mary Kay filled my every thought. First, I asked everyone I *knew* to have a party. The next day, I decided I had to open up my trolling area, so I made it my goal to ask every woman

I *saw* to have a party. I would stop the lady on the bus, ask the checker at the store, intercept the policewoman on the beat. I mean, no one was off limits. Momma needed some recruits to create her empire, because it wasn't going to build itself.

I was a devoted believer in my ability to grow my business and become independently wealthy, but no matter how hard I sold it—and I sold it hard—all I did was lose friends and alienate people. (Now there's a book I could write.) My passion just didn't translate to cosmetic salvation. And soon, I was so overwhelmed with rejection that I didn't even want to leave my house. I was convinced that leaving the house meant I had to sell, sell, sell—but that was sending everyone running, running, running.

I ended up closing up shop just two months into it, claiming emotional exhaustion from too much rejection and embarrassment. Where had I gone wrong?

I was reminded of this season yesterday while I sat in my chiropractor's office. On the wall, he had a big sign that said, "Refer a friend to our practice and you could win a $1,000 shopping spree!"

I thought, "A shopping spree would give me some serious chiropractic relief!" So I scanned my Rolodex—kickin' it old school again!—looking for people I could refer to my chiropractor. And then I remembered my Mary Kay days. Those days of desperately wanting to infect another woman with the glory of building her own business, all the while smoothing out her wrinkles. Suddenly, I realized that with the right incentive, I'd tell everyone and anyone I know about anything.

Then I thought, "It's too bad God doesn't offer cash prize incentives to the church every time we talk about Jesus. I'd be an unstoppable force for the Lord!" There I go exposing myself again—all in the name of healing and a little humor.

> *What we enjoy, we glorify. We talk about and evangelize whatever it is we love.*

What is it James 5:16 says? "Confess your sins to one another...that you may be healed." Yeah, that's it. Let the healing begin.

Listen, when it comes to hope and building my empire, I may be a bit of an extremist, but I figure, *go overwhelmed or go home*. More than one person in my life has annoyingly whined, "Moderation, Hayley. Moderation." And I've considered the moderation thing, but then I firmly walked away from it based on how overwhelming it was.

That said, I don't think moderation is meant to be the number one goal in our lives. I believe we were *made* to be overwhelmed. That would explain why I go from one state of overwhelmedness to the next—it's just a natural state of being.

So if you aren't overwhelmed by something, then maybe it's time to be! (That's my new motto.)

THOUGHTS TO PONDER

Are you overwhelmed by something?

If you are, then what is the fruit of that preoccupation? Is this state of overwhelmedness making you more peaceful, hopeful, joyful, and free? Is it opening up your world to possibility? Is it drawing people to you who want what you have? When we are overwhelmed, those around us know it because of our fruit. And this fruit, just like the fruit we eat, points to the type of tree that's growing it.

What type of tree would you say produces the fruit you have in your life?

What type of fruit do you most crave in your life that you don't have right now? (For example, peace, rest, love, self-control, faithfulness, joy, and so on.)

What do you know or imagine you would enjoy being overwhelmed with?

What does God want you to be overwhelmed with?

A catechism is just a simple question and answer that the early church practiced. One old catechism that the Catholic fathers agreed was a good thing for all believers to know went like this:

Question: Why did God create us?
(Any ideas? It's really a dreamy answer.)
Answer: God created us to enjoy Him and to glorify Him forever.

And one follows the other: what we enjoy, we glorify. We talk about and evangelize whatever it is we love.

What do you spend the most time talking about? That will reveal your heart's affections.

I love shopping—I really do—and that's why I was compelled to refer everyone I knew to my chiropractor. But as I thought about my impetus for reaching out, it grieved me that I would be so easily baited into doing something that scares me—telling other people about something they haven't asked me about first—just for money. Sure, mentioning my chiropractor's name to someone who asks me if I know a good one is easy, but cold-calling someone to tell them the good news about my pain relief, and theirs too, is not my idea of a good time. Yet I was willing to do it for the money. Ugh!

I am readily willing to talk about the things that consume me, those things that overwhelm me either for the good or for the bad. Talking about it gives me a much-needed sense of relief and completion.

Do you find many subjects competing for your conversational attention and energy? Maybe that's because you have become overwhelmed with so much. Yet, I believe we weren't meant to become overwhelmed to distraction but to devotion.

26

I'M LIKE THE FAT IN A CHEESE STICK

I remember the first thing I ever learned about God. It came in the form of a bedtime prayer. You've probably said it before too. It goes like this:

Now I lay me down to sleep
I pray the Lord my soul to keep

And here is where it gets really good for small children:

If I should DIE before I wake

Wait a minute, what? There's a chance I'm going to die before morning? So, you bet, I'd better...

Pray the Lord my soul to take.

Each night my sweet, unchurched mother would lead me to the feet of Jesus by telling me that I better pray that

God would keep my soul, because my body might not make it through the night. Hallelujah! And I wonder where my warped sense of who God is came from.

My second most memorable childhood interaction with God was at a children's Vacation Bible School. I'm not sure why I was there, since my parents only went to church at Easter and Christmas, but for some reason they had dumped me off there. All I remember is sitting in a little chair with a bunch of kids around, being asked to close my eyes in prayer. As I did, one of the adults grabbed a little toy out of my tiny hands, telling me passive-aggressively that, "If you hold that toy, it's like you are praying to it! Are you praying to it?"

I shook my little head no.

"Then give it to me!" She ripped it out of my hands.

And yet another inaccurate view of who God is drilled into my developing mind.

By the time I was in high school, my heart was fertile ground for the teachings of the angry and frustrated father who taught at my private Catholic school, telling me that I was so far from acceptable to Jesus that I'd never find my salvation in Him.

By the time I graduated, all I knew about the Lord was that He could save my soul before I woke, but only if I confessed my sins in the Catholic Church—at least according to this possibly well-intentioned but definitely misguided priest. And because my parents weren't Catholic and never took me to this one and only place where I could do my confessing, I was sure that I'd never be seen, let alone loved, by such a holy God.

For all four years in high school, I used to watch the old televangelist Jimmy Swaggart, tears streaming down my face, as he'd say:

"Yes, I want Jesus!"

"Yes, I believe He is the Son of God."

"Yes, I want Him to come into my life."

Every Sunday for four years I accepted Christ, because I thought I had lost Him during the week. Yes, this was my early Christian education. My ideas about God were a haphazard col-

> *When God overwhelms your former view of the world with His glorious goodness, you can't help but shout it from the rooftops.*

lection of half-truths and hopes that would never come true. So, when a Christian boy that worked at the limousine shop where I worked asked me why I cussed like a sailor when I professed to be a Christian, I told him, "I'm not good enough for God. So, I figure, if I'm going to hell, I might as well have fun on the way."

And this was the moment when the veil was lifted. This was the exact point when I finally saw God for who He really is, and not some dictatorial deity designed to keep children in their place. This young man told me one thing and one thing only about God. It wasn't much, but it was everything I needed to trust that the Lord would keep my soul until I woke: he told me about God's amazing grace. Then he opened up his beat-up old Bible, all underlined and dog-eared, and turned it toward me with his finger on Romans 10:9. "Read this," he said.

"If you confess with your mouth that Jesus is Lord and believe in your heart that God raised him from the dead, you will be saved." I read these words like a starving kitten tasting its first bowl of milk.

"You have got to be kidding me," I howled as I put both fists on my hips. "How come no one ever told me this?" I meowed.

My coworker, of course, didn't have an answer. But he gave me his old Bible and I began to lap it up page by page, hour by hour, day by day. And as I did, my idea of God grew bigger and bigger, and I started to see Him for who He really is. I started to see that I had Him all wrong. He was a merciful God who sent His Son to die, not because of how perfect I was, but because of how perfect He is. He wasn't absent and power-less; He was omnipresent and omniscient. And He knew me, yet He still loved me.

Yes, seeing the true love of God is what saved my life. From that moment on, I was overwhelmed by His love for me. I mean, I was saturated in it like the fat in a cheese stick fried in fat. I was like saturated fat! Every inch of me was focused on Him, and I knew what I had to do. I had to tell the world! They needed to know this God—this God who I'd searched so long for. So, I set about doing just that.

When God overwhelms your former view of the world with His glorious goodness, you can't help but shout it from the rooftops. Even if you weren't saved as late in life as I was, there are always moments when God shows you the depth of your darkness by revealing the glory of His light. In those moments, He threatens to overwhelm you, and all you have to do is to surrender to the fact that someone has given you an extravagant gift that you don't deserve and just accept it. Not accepting it does no harm to anyone but yourself. And who are you to say no to the God of the universe?

THOUGHTS TO PONDER

Do you remember the first time you were overwhelmed by the love of God?

You were made to be overwhelmed by His love, so it shouldn't be hard, but it does require a mind set on seeing through the darkness and into His loving eyes. It requires us to look away from the distractions that shout for our attention and to focus on the One who whispers His love.

If you had to tell someone the most overwhelming thing about what God has done for you, what would it be?

Where does God fit into that thing or situation that overwhelms most of your day?

What is your number one goal for today? Is it to be overwhelmed by God? How would you accomplish that?

Being overwhelmed by God comes easily to the new believer, because humans are easily consumed by newness. Newness alerts our senses to the goodness of a thing. But over time, that newness wears off, which means we have to continue to remind ourselves of what He has done and who He is.

A. W. Tozer wrote a book that reminds me of these things every time I pick it up: *The Knowledge of the Holy.* If you would like to dive deeper into goodness, find someone to disciple you, ask others what God has done for them, read books like the one by Tozer, and fellowship every chance you get with anyone who will talk to you about your God.

27

THE YEAR MY MOM
MOVED OUT

In the fall of 2016, my mother moved out. I had grown accustomed to her living with us in our home. We ate together, and we spent the days running errands, doing homeschool activities, and having fun. She was our constant companion—my daughter's and mine.

My glory was always more glorious when I could share it with her. And my grief more healing when she recognized my pain.

Devastation threatened me for a moment when she left us in the dark of the night. We had planned for her departure, and we had prayed for a smooth journey, but still the darkness made it more ominous and fatal in my mind. My heart was weighted down like a water balloon under a boulder, threatening to burst and disappear into oblivion. But the grief competed with the relief and joy I also felt, and was somehow subdued into a cleansing flow of saltwater from my face.

You see, where she was going was far better for her than it was for me, so the selfish part of me wanted to yank on her nightgown and pull her back. To tell her, "No, don't go. We can make this thing work." But the love I felt for her trumped the needs I had for myself, and so I was comforted by her comfort, soothed by her salvation, and at peace with her departure.

> When I began to study God and to sense this size difference, what had seemed big and overwhelming before suddenly seemed insignificant.

While she lived here, she was trapped—trapped by her own physical and mental limitations. She was a child being raised by her own child, and she was a woman who was aware of her unawareness, and both these things grieved her. She wanted out. She wanted to walk without help, to know where she was, and to be joyful and complete—none of which she could have while she remained with us. So, that is why I could say goodbye.

Ten years ago, I wouldn't have been able to say the same thing. Ten years ago, I wasn't as certain as I am now of God's goodness, mercy, or sovereignty, so I am thankful for God's timing. And in the fall of 2016, my mother stopped living on earth and started living in heaven. She went from the chains of old age to the freedom of flight in the presence of God's pure light. She graduated. She reached her goal of salvation and she was ready to go home.

Last week, my daughter asked me why I didn't still weep for Gigi, why I seemed to be OK talking about her, laughing at the things she laughed at, and remembering how she loved the Chinese buffet and Sonic Drive-In. I told her that I wasn't lost in sorrow because I was certain of God's sovereignty. (Yes, my ten-year-old understands words like *sovereignty*; makes a momma proud!)

You see, without God's sovereignty, we are forever at the whim of environment, and at the mercy of malevolent human—and inhuman—beings. But His sovereignty gives meaning to everything, even our suffering. From facing disappointment to disaster, knowing that God's omnipotence, omniscience, and omnipresence are equaled only by His infiniteness and love gives us the freedom to joyfully allow the floor to slip out from underneath us and send us plummeting toward the ground. For we know that we aren't falling, but riding in His righteous right hand.

So many times, we become overwhelmed with the sorrows and suffering of life because we forget that God is eternal. We forget that He goes on forever, in both directions of time, and that not only He, but all of His attributes, live on in infinity. We've all heard it so many times: God is love. But sometimes I fail to remember that He isn't the kind of love I experience from mere mortals, the kind that is fickle and conditional. God's love is infinite, never-ending, going in front of and behind me forever and ever. And this infinite nature applies to all of who He is. His omnipotence is forever. His omniscience, His grace, His mercy—it all has no end and no beginning.

From this perspective, the things that overwhelm us are minuscule. They are a bump on the bum of a mosquito by comparison. They look big up close, but from where God sits, they are cellular in size.

When I began to study the attributes of God and to sense this size difference, what had seemed big and overwhelming before suddenly seemed insignificant; it was useful only insofar as it revealed more of Him to me. We humanoids have a hard time remembering, or even conceiving, of the infiniteness of God. The fact that all that He is has no bounds is probably as easy for me to understand as it is for a child to understand how her dreams could come true: both are impossible to know, yet wonderful to imagine.

God never runs out of His being. He never stops being faithful, merciful, just. He never gets to the end of His omnipotence or omnipresence. That's why the psalmist says there is nowhere he can hide from God's presence, nowhere God will not hold him, nothing God does not know. When I get overwhelmed with the world, I remind myself of this overwhelming love and of this God who has love without bounds and all the power of the universe. For me, whatever God in His infinite wisdom believes is best is far more overwhelming than the finite problems in my life. In His infinity, I find protection and purpose.

THOUGHTS TO PONDER

Sometimes we take the attributes of God for granted. We give lip service to His "Godness," all the while fearing in our hearts that He just isn't enough—not enough power, not enough love, not enough faithfulness. It's human nature to fear this way, because the only thing we have to compare God to is other human beings, and none of them compare. But the more we devote ourselves to the study of who God is, the more we become naturally overwhelmed by what we learn.

Which attribute of God overwhelms you the most? (Some examples to consider: love, mercy, omniscience, omnipotence, wisdom, goodness, faithfulness, justice, holiness, grace, sovereignty, self-existence, mercy, patience, kindness, and truthfulness.)

When you are overwhelmed, which attribute(s) of God do you think you might be forgetting?

I challenge you to pick an attribute today and study it. Look into who God is in this one area. The further you dive into who God is, the more you will become overwhelmed by Him, and the more this world—with all of its worries—will pale by comparison.

And, speaking of *comparison*...

Earlier, I talked about the danger of comparison, but that was the danger of comparing yourself to another of God's creations. Comparing yourself to God, on the other hand, is a freeing exercise—because, in it, you find your powerlessness—and His power in your weakness. In other words, in your weakness is where you find strength. In recognizing His holiness over your own, you realize that He is a better God than you ever could be—and because He is all of those things I've listed, He can be trusted with your every living moment.

Can you trust a God like this to manage your day? To choose your path? To fight your battles and to give you rest?

Ask Him today to set you free from the mission of me and to set you firmly down in His amazing goodness. In this way, you can become like a child kept safely in her father's house, certain that nothing bad will ever come to her with her daddy present . . . and He is always present.

28

THE ELEVATOR OPERATOR OF DEATH

Don't tell anyone, but I don't trust builders of buildings taller than two stories. It's not that I think they are evil or incompetent; I just know that they are human and prone to make mistakes. And if a guy is going to make a mistake, I don't want it to be the person who laid the 160th floor that I'm standing on, you know what I mean?

So, when we took our daughter to Seattle and she wanted to go to the top of the Space Needle, I was afraid for my life. As we swooshed in on the space-age monorail, I looked up, both hands on the window, and cringed like a little schoolgirl. The view from the base of this monolith was dizzying, and just looking up at it I almost tipped over. The thought of looking down from the top was threatening to come up my throat and pour onto the concrete. But like a good mommy, I got my ticket, and handed it to the elevator operator of death.

As we went up, my stomach churned, and when the doors

> *I determined a long time ago not to let fear control my actions. Fear does not dictate what I do.*

opened onto the observation deck, I wanted to grab the handrail and stay inside. But when I came to the realization that the elevator was just going to plummet back to the ground, I jumped out and frantically searched for the most stable part of the needle I could find. Meanwhile, everyone else wanted to look over the edge like a bunch of thrill-seekers. I slowly slid my feet in the direction of danger, while the rest of them walked around as if their movement wouldn't tip the thing to one side and throw us all off.

They clearly don't understand physics like I do!

But then I saw it—the view from on high. It was breathtaking. And suddenly I forgot my fear. I grabbed my phone and started posing for selfies. This feat had to be documented!

The sun was about to touch the sound as dark rain clouds formed in the south. It was a heart-stirring view, and I couldn't peel my eyes away. By the end of our visit, I was actually happy that I had gone to the top and looked down at the rest of the world.

I'm like that with roller coasters too. I hate, *hate* the idea of roller coasters. As I wait in line, fear grips my throat, sending my feet flapping wildly as they attempt fruitlessly to run away. When it's time to board, I walk to the little car like a death-row prisoner headed to the chair; then they strap me into the seat that will roll me to my death. Before the first ascent, I am in the pits of terror just thinking about how I am at the mercy of this mechanical monstrosity. I get flashbacks of that one video where people plummet to their deaths in a malfunctioning machine, and I want to run the other way. But this senseless sense of overwhelming fear is replaced by overwhelming excitement as we roll at breakneck speed down the first hill.

Once the ride is done and we glide back into the station, the first words out of my mouth are, "Let's do it again!"

You might wonder how I got onto the coaster in the first place, as overwhelmed with fear as I was. That is a good thing to wonder. But let me tell you my secret. I determined a long time ago not to let fear control my actions. Fear does not dictate what I do. Instead, I decided not to live under the deception that I can somehow control my date and time of death (which is futile, as that has already been decided by my Creator). So, whether riding roller coasters or flying on planes that I'm sure will crash, I have decided to always tell fear to be quiet—and to do that, I must defy it any chance I get. Eventually, it gets the idea and gives up trying to control me. (Although, honestly, I haven't ridden enough rollers to claim coaster victory yet. But I will get there!)

At any rate, I see this law at work whenever I am overwhelmed: the only thing that can save me from overwhelm is something more overwhelming. And since there is truly nothing more overwhelming than God, I am set free from those things that used to control me as long as I am with Him. That means I can ride the roller coaster of life with an often fearless reliance on the One who created both the hills and the valleys, the flips and the rolls, and the corkscrew and the dangle. I'm not totally free of fear—it still rears its hideous head from time to time—but in most cases, I can slap some lipstick on it and just laugh at its colorful but contemptible kisser.

> *God's power overwhelms any other power in the universe.*

THOUGHTS TO PONDER

Have you ever felt the sentence of death? That is, have you ever been sure that this struggle would kill you before you could beat it?

There are a lot of things in life designed to prove that you just can't do it, but thankfully they were also designed to prove that God can. In Genesis, Joseph told his brothers who sold him into slavery, "You intended to harm me, but God intended it for good to accomplish what is now being done, the saving of many lives" (Genesis 50:20, NIV). No matter how terrible something looks, God always has a plan to deliver us. We have to look to that delivery instead of to our doom.

What scares you?

How does this fear control your choices and actions?

Consider God's love for you and His ability to do whatever He wants. How could He be working in the dangerous and deadly parts of your life for His glory and your good?

Can you remember times in your past when you thought you couldn't make it through? How did God prove Himself in those moments?

Job 14:5 tells us that our days are determined by God. He has already decided exactly how long you will live. That means He will keep you safe in His arms until that day, but it also means that you can't escape that day with one moment of fear or irrational self-protection. You cannot hedge the bets of your life with being overly protective of yourself or those you love. But when you realize that God's love and plans are far greater than your own, when you recognize that His wisdom far outweighs yours, then you can sit back and relax when the kids leave the house for the first time, when someone you love moves to Africa to serve the poor, and whenever scary things are asked of you. You can rest in the knowledge that God can be trusted no matter the outcome.

God's power overwhelms any other power in the universe.

29

I FOUGHT THE LAW AND THE LAW WON

Many years ago, I was pulling off the freeway into downtown Nashville, when suddenly there was a policeman standing in front of me, waving at me to pull over. I felt so naughty, like I had just escaped prison and the warden had found me and was about to drag me back to the hole. I was shocked as I obediently pulled onto the side street where he was standing.

What had I done? All I did was get off the freeway, stop at the red light, and then proceed to turn right after checking that there was no traffic. Sounds perfectly legal to me.

"Did you know you can't turn right on a red at that light?" he said in his toughest cop voice.

"No, I didn't," I innocently responded.

He looked at me like a father who'd just heard his daughter say, "I didn't know I couldn't feed my broccoli to the dog."

He smirked. "Sure, you didn't."

I was shocked. I wasn't lying—honest! And I can prove it! "I'm a Christian!" I shouted at him indignantly.

My friend in the passenger seat, who was also a Christian, said (much to my surprise), "What does that have to do with anything?"

As I turned to him, I confidently proclaimed, "It proves everything! Christians don't lie!"

Nope, it didn't work on either of them.

I really believed that my faith proved my innocence and honesty. How could they not understand that I was overwhelmed by God and would never, ever break the law!

> You may deeply believe a thing, but when your actions don't prove it, they can become suspicious.

No matter how hard you try, you can't always convince the world of the true state of your heart. You may deeply believe a thing, but when your actions don't prove it, they can become suspicious. And that's the worst feeling—to be doubted—especially by someone who has the power to punish you when you fail to prove yourself. My life has quite a rap sheet of being doubted: people have doubted my love, my honesty, my abilities, and my faith. Let me tell you, if you don't already know, that being doubted hurts; you come away from every encounter feeling isolated and alone, as if no one truly believes or understands you. It's like a kind of solitary confinement.

And that's why it is so overwhelming when you find out that God knows all your ways—that He knows a word before it is on your tongue, that He discerns your thoughts from afar, and that He never, ever misunderstands your heart. As humanoids, we yearn to be known. We want a connection that is unmistakable and faithful. And when we find that, we never want to let it go.

That's how it was for me when I first met Jesus. I was so amazed by His knowledge of me that I wept. I remember reading the Book of Romans from the driver's seat of my black limousine while my customers partied their hearts out at the club. Under the cab's reading light, I devoured the truth that was me—it was all me, this stuff that Paul had said. I wanted to be good, I really did, but I just couldn't seem to do it. I worked so hard, for so many years, to be good enough for God, and it wasn't until I was driving limousines for a living that I found out—in the dark of night and in the midst of sin—that He was more merciful than I had ever known. It overwhelms me even today when I think about how Paul expressed exactly what was in my own heart:

> So I find it to be a law that when I want to do
> right, evil lies close at hand. For I delight in
> the law of God, in my inner being, but I see in
> my members another law waging war against
> the law of my mind and making me captive
> to the law of sin that dwells in my members.
> Wretched man that I am! Who will deliver
> me from this body of death? Thanks be to
> God through Jesus Christ our Lord! So then,
> I myself serve the law of God with my mind,
> but with my flesh I serve the law of sin. There
> is therefore now no condemnation for those
> who are in Christ Jesus. (Romans 7:21–8:1)

Those words, "There is therefore now no condemnation for those who are in Christ Jesus" are at the very heart of the gospel. And they represent the single most important fact for the believer—that we are accepted by a perfect God despite our sinful past, present, and future. This idea is too wonderful for me, too big for me to understand, but I know how desperately I need it. And so I embrace it, because without this truth, there is no hope for me. I cannot *not* sin; it is just plain impossible. I am going to hurt you, I am going to break the law, I am going to do what I don't want to do. I am a sinner—but I am saved by His amazing grace!

THOUGHTS TO PONDER

For years, I believed that the only way I could improve myself—the only way to stop making mistakes, to be perfect, to do what I wanted to do—was to work harder. Like a hamster running in her wheel, I believed that my work was getting me somewhere, but I was actually staying in the same place while my little legs pretended to make progress. This constant need to advance while remaining stationary was life-consuming, and gives me a better understanding of why hamsters nervously chew and constantly twitch. A lack of forward movement will make anyone crazy.

In what way have you tried to improve or prove yourself?

What sins in your life have you been unable to break free from?

Romans 6:15 says, "Sin will have no dominion over you, since you are not under law but under grace." What does this mean to you? To your inability to be perfect?

Are you willing to accept His grace today?

PastorHoney always tells me that you can never out-sin God's grace. There will always be more grace than there is sin. Can you believe that? No wonder we call it amazing!

When you become overwhelmed by the mess you've made of your life, remember that Jesus came to seek and save the messy, messed-up people who recognize that the depth of their difference comes from Him. He came for people who are honest about how weak they truly are and want nothing more than for Him to lift them up and dust them off.

The entire message of the Bible is this gospel truth that no one can be perfect, and that's why the Father had to send the Son to save us. No matter how long you've loved God, you still have to remind yourself of the gospel facts: His grace is more than you will ever need. You are loved by Him. And because of that love, He will never leave you the way you are right now, but will bring you through into His marvelous light.

30

YOU'RE A BAD GIRL, WILMA JEAN

I have a little dog that looks like a poster pup for the Humane Society.

Long ears stick up above her thin, bristled curls that can't seem to agree on which direction to go. Her eyes are so big that I'm not sure her eyelids have given up trying to cover them. Let's just say she's irresistible to a mother and father who love her as if they themselves had created her in the passion of the night.

Her name is Wilma. Wilma Jean if she's naughty.

And believe me, she's naughty. But she's just so "zisstable" (that's Wilma talk for *irresistible*) that this is usually how things play out: I'm standing at the kitchen sink, intently moving dirty plates around so I can find the garbage disposal. Wilma approaches from my right, looks at me, sees I'm busy, then jumps up onto the dining room chair. After another quick confirmation that I still don't see her, she leaps onto the table

> *It's overwhelming to manage all my sins, keeping them under wraps and under control—and after a while, they naturally add to the overwhelming feeling that it's hard just to be me.*

and begins looking through crumbs and crafts to find a treasure. I turn, just in time to catch her in the act, and screech in my best Marge Simpson voice, "Wilma Jean! What are you doing on that table?"

Now, you'd think she would jump off like any sensible dog caught red-handed. But instead, she starts out with a tremor, and while shaking, she tucks her tail between her legs and puts down her back end slowly. She then lowers her head to look at me with her signature puppy dog eyes, and, at the same time, her ears lie down and silently plead for mercy. Then, finally, she tilts her head and tacitly confesses her sins. Who says dogs don't cry? (Cue "In the Arms of the Angel.")

At this point, I'm so overwhelmed by her broken and contrite heart that I cannot despise her. I pick her up in my arms and pull her close to me as I start kissing her on the face saying, "You're a bad girl, Wilma Jean, but I love you anyway."

Wilma Jean knows how to own up to her own inability to do what she knows she needs to do. It's as if she has figured out that there is no condemnation for those who are in our home. And she's right: if she confesses her sins, we are faithful and just to forgive her of her sins. And if I'm so faithful and just to my oversized drowned rat, how much more faithful and just will my God be?

Ha ha! It's an analogy! But you probably caught that.

Sometimes I doubt the father's ability or desire to forgive me, so I move my sins to one side of my life and keep dusting and organizing them like they're porcelain knick-knacks I've collected over the years, and refusing to admit that they're really just little piles of poo that I've dropped and refused to clean up. It's overwhelming to manage all my sins, keeping them under wraps and under control—and after a while, they naturally add to the overwhelming feeling that it's hard just to be me.

I remember a few years ago when I suddenly realized that I was harsh and judgmental. I guess turnabout's fair play, because boy was I harsh and judgmental with myself for a change.

"How can I be such a jerk *and* be a Christian?" I cried to my husband.

He assured me that it was easy, and I quickly said, "Then I need a change!" God had turned on the lights to show me my ugly self, and like Eve, I wanted to sew a bikini and hide behind the bushes. I didn't understand how I could know so much and get it so wrong. And I couldn't see how God could forgive me.

I think it's easier for me to see salvation for others than for myself sometimes. Must have to do with my inherent sense of pride: "I ought to be better than this," I subconsciously reason, and because I ought to know better, I don't deserve grace. But when others are contrite and confessing their sins, I am the first to

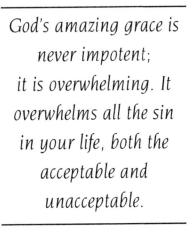

God's amazing grace is never impotent; it is overwhelming. It overwhelms all the sin in your life, both the acceptable and unacceptable.

THOUGHTS TO PONDER

Some may say that we are too free with grace, that we take advantage of it and use it as an escape clause into the world of sin. But while that can be true, in many cases grace feels underwhelming, if not impotent. Like a chronic dieter, we tend to hold onto the lie that if we just work harder, things will improve. But God's amazing grace is never impotent; it is overwhelming. It overwhelms all the sin in your life, both the acceptable and unacceptable.

Unacceptable sins are those sins that you hate in your life. Those things that you wish you could be done with because they are so ugly and cause so much pain.

"Acceptable" sins are those traits in your life that you are comfortable with because you know you are powerless to change them, simply because they are a part of your personality.

But both kinds of sin need salvation, and both can receive the healing salve of God's grace when we are willing to confess them and to trust that even those habitual sins that seem to be a part of us can be changed by the power of His love.

What are some unacceptable sins that you'd like to be done with?

Look for any "acceptable" sins in your life. Sins like coveting, jealousy, gluttony, laziness, prayerless-ness, isolation, and selfishness. Can you trust God to change those areas of your life?

Do you believe that God can forgive any of your sins? If not, then what Scripture supports that belief?

In 1 John 1:9-10, it says, "If we confess our sins, he is faithful and just to forgive us our sins and to cleanse us from all unrighteousness. If we say we have not sinned, we make him a liar, and his word is not in us."

In an effort to never call God a liar, both in private and public, I have determined to be free with the confession of my sins. Not because I am proud of them, but because I agree with His Word that all have sinned and will continue to sin, which means I need a constant supply of His grace. Only when I have stopped sinning can I say that I no longer need His grace.

31

AN OVERWHELMING CONCLUSION

When I first started going to church, all I knew I had to do was get up in the morning, kiss my boyfriend good-bye, and drive to the suburbs. After that, I didn't know anything about anything. Oh, sure, I knew I was saved—at least I was pretty sure. I knew that God loved me, though I couldn't imagine why. And I knew I needed to learn more about Him before I could be sure of anything. But that's all I knew. I had no other to-do list for my Sunday than to show up and let the learning begin.

But going from limo driver to small-church parishioner was a jolt to the system. For example, I knew one needed to dress up for church, so every Sunday, I put on my nicest dress-up clothes: a black lace skirt (which could be mistaken for a wide belt), a black vest (without anything underneath except a sexy black bra), black stockings (which, of course, had a garter belt), and high heels. I then jumped into my yellow convertible Bug,

> *What overwhelms us on this earth is not nearly as overwhelming as the Creator of this earth.*

music blaring, and hit the road. Praise Jesus! I was sexy and ready to learn.

Week after week, I would walk through those doors oblivious to all of the stares of disbelief, intent on only one thing: getting more information about this God whom I knew so little about. And every week, a young woman who agreed to walk with me through the journey greeted me and patiently answered all my questions before, during, and after the service.

The more I knew about God, the more I fell in love. The more I saw of Him, the more He intrigued me and the more I wanted Him. I was in love, and it was a burning kind of love; the kind that was kindled in the fire that raged deep in my soul for the God who would accept a sinner such as me. And the deeper I fell into the heat, the less I wanted of this world. And so my to-do list went from ...

1. Get a better job.
2. Keep my boyfriend.
3. Find true happiness.

To ...

1. Love God with all my heart, soul, mind, and strength.

And that meant there had to be change in my life.

The first change was the boyfriend. He expected my faith to be a passing fancy, and when it stuck with a vengeance, he couldn't stand the heat, not to mention the constant talk about God. So he took himself out of the equation.

Then the job got some attention. Driving men to strip clubs and couples to inspiration point was not a healthy environment for this God-lover. But God made the move for me: I was "laid off" after starting a Bible study in the office, which my boss did not appreciate.

So, with my boyfriend gone, job taken, and life changed, I couldn't have been happier. I was suddenly free—free to do one thing and one thing only: to love God.

Where would He take me? What would we do? I didn't know, but I didn't worry over it; I just held on for the ride. And as I made God my life, He took me from the pit to the pinnacle—from being a struggling artist to a thriving follower of Christ—in two short years. And in that time, the things that had once overwhelmed me had been replaced by my overwhelming God, who taught me that life is a whole different ballgame when your entire focus is His mission not your own.

What overwhelms us on this earth is not nearly as overwhelming as the Creator of this earth. His love, His mercy, His presence, His grace—they are overwhelming. And when we remind ourselves of this fact, and when we return to our first love, we remember that whatever is overwhelming us in the moment is nothing in comparison to who God is.

Yes, there will be difficult times. We will suffer in this world, but we must take heart because He is our God and He is overwhelming.

You were made to be overwhelmed, but not by worry, stress, fear or doubt. So I pray that this journey through the rearview mirror of my life has lifted your spirit, shown you parts of yourself you were unfamiliar with, and opened your heart to the love of the Father. If it has, then there is only one thing for you to do now, and that's to love Him. Love Him with all of your heart, soul, mind, and strength—and when you do, you will find that loving your neighbor isn't as difficult, trying, stressful, or embarrassing as it once was.

If you are tired of being overwhelmed by life, then choose to make the mission of God your number one focus. Allow His mission to become more important than your own and nothing will derail your goal to bring Him glory. That is His mission—that you find love, joy, peace, patience, kindness, goodness, faithfulness, gentleness and self-control. And you will be overflowing with this fruit of His Spirit as you embrace His mission as your own.

I am praying for you today, friend. Praying that these words find you ready to embrace the love and mission of God, and to enter into the life of a woman overwhelmed with grace.

Looking for a way to dig deeper into the

A Woman Overwhelmed

message and engage in conversation with others on the subject?

Want to learn what Mary can teach us about being overwhelmed?

HAYLEY DiMARCO

Discover the ultimate stress reliever by experiencing the overwhelming grace and love of God!

Find freedom in becoming overwhelmed with who God is—by learning to focus on what we know about God so that we can hold onto faith even when it seems that all is lost.

The six-week *A Woman Overwhelmed* Bible study **walks through the story of Mary, the mother of Jesus,** offering biblical and practical application related to aspects of life that can make us feel overwhelmed. Dig into the Old and New Testaments and hear relatable modern-day stories as we learn how to be consumed with the mission of God rather than the "mission of me."

COMPONENTS:
Participant Workbook | 9781501839924
Leader Guide | 9781501839948
DVD | 9781501839962
Leader Kit | 9781501839979

Get Session 1 for Free at: AbingdonWomen.com/HayleyDiMarco